Two-Wheeled
Wind Therapy

Road Dog Publications was formed in 2010 as an imprint dedicated to publishing the best in books on motorcycling and adventure travel. Visit us at www.roaddogpub.com.

No part of this book may be reproduced by any means, nor transmitted, nor translated into a machine language, without the written permission of the publishers.

ISBN 978-1-890623-80-7
Library of Congress Control Number: 2021938716

An Imprint of Lost Classics Book Company
This book also available in eBook format at online booksellers. ISBN 978-1-890623-81-4

Two-Wheeled Wind Therapy

My Journey Finding Confidence, Joy, and Hope After Surviving Cancer, Divorce, and a Pandemic

by

Kathleen Terner

Publisher
Lake Wales, Florida

Dedicated to
*Kathleen Bufford, Michelle Martin, Kathy Nesper,
Beth Soloway, and Linda Terner. Thank you for being there for
me when it mattered the most.*

About the Author

A respectable, middle-aged mother of three adored adult children and math teacher by day, Kathleen Terner secretly delights in being called "bad-ass" by other bikers, hotel reservationists, and colleagues—and she's earned the title! Her love affair with motorcycling took her over 100,000 miles through forty-eight states in less than six and a half years, first on the back of a bike and then driving her own, even after a battle with throat cancer and a divorce that left her without a riding partner.

Just two years after getting her motorcycle endorsement, Kathleen set out on an eight-week, solo cross-country trip. Initially apprehensive about traveling alone, she discovered an inner strength she'd never known she had, thriving on the solitude she had once feared. Her confidence in her skills as a motorcyclist burgeoned as she successfully completed two certified endurance rides and dealt with mechanical issues, extreme weather, and some of the United States' most technically challenging roads.

Kathleen credits her ability to overcome obstacles to the support of old and new friends, the "wind therapy" from her miles on the road, and her personal faith. Grateful for her newfound joy after years of hardship, she is dedicated to encouraging others not to give up when faced with seemingly insurmountable difficulties.

For more information on Kathleen and to see photos appearing in this book in full color visit kathleenterner.com.

CONTENTS

Testing out the touring bags in Seaside, Oregon, before the trip

CHAPTER ONE

NOTHING SHORT OF A MIRACLE

"I just want to say 'thank you.'" The man's words barely registered in my consciousness. After all, I was absorbed in my pre-ride routine—putting on my helmet first, then the goggles, then the gloves. The date was June 10, 2020. I had just finished going on a lunch ride with my local Harley Owners Group (HOG) and had stopped briefly at the Latus dealership to make plans to ride with another friend toward the Oregon coast. I hadn't had a significant conversation with anyone at the dealership and was planning to get in a couple hundred more miles on the bike before it got dark. But then I saw the biker's motorcycle boots in my peripheral vision and looked up. He continued, "My wife saw you drive up with your touring bags on the bike and said, 'I want to be like that.' You inspired her to become more comfortable on her bike."

I was shocked. At that particular moment, I didn't think I was the kind of person who could inspire anyone. Just a few months earlier I had lost the ability to speak, eat, or drink—side effects from aggressive chemotherapy and radiation treatments for the throat cancer that had threatened to kill me. I was finally able to speak and eat solid food again but still had difficulty chewing, swallowing, and tasting. In addition to my physical struggles, I was also feeling like a failure because I had just finalized a second divorce.

I had only recently started riding my bike again, after months on powerful narcotics for the pain from my cancer treatments. It had taken weeks to get the bike ready for summer travel, partially because I had changed so much physically from the cancer. At five feet two inches tall and 135 pounds before my treatments began, I had considered myself of average build. But after seven and a half weeks of daily radiation treatments and three rounds of chemotherapy, I had dropped twenty-five pounds and had trouble comfortably reaching the handlebars on my bike. My chaps no longer fit, and I hadn't had the hardware or luggage to go anywhere on my own. I had just figured out how to re-configure my bike with a new seat, rack, sissy bar, and touring bags and had left the bags on for the ride that day because I was still learning how to properly detach and attach them. So it was nothing short of a miracle that I was planning to leave shortly on the biggest adventure of my life—an eight-week, solo cross-country trip from Oregon to Washington, DC, and back.

When I had driven into the dealership to park the bike and contact friends about riding more that day, I had only briefly noticed the man and his wife in the parking lot. She was dropping him off with all his gear, and he appeared to be picking up his bike after it had been serviced. When he gave me such a nice compliment, I was initially speechless. But then I remembered what it was like to drive a bike for the first time and how, for me and some other riders, it can be a terrifying experience. I gave the man my name and suggested his wife connect with me on Facebook. I told him I would be delighted to support and encourage her in any way possible because riding was such a blessing to me. She never contacted me, but it planted a seed in my head that maybe there were other riders out there I could encourage and inspire, helping them to experience the tremendous joy I felt while on my bike.

Although I had not learned to drive my own bike until age fifty-two, just two years before my encounter at the dealership, I took to it with a level of passion that surprised even myself. It was exhilarating and empowering to direct and guide so much horsepower up hills, around curves, and down straightaways. I felt I could express an inner strength not normally reflected by my slight physique. Riding a bike also allowed me to experience the world around me with all five of my senses— feeling the sun on my back, smelling the seaweed at the ocean, tasting the salty air, hearing the waves, and seeing the deep blue water. The rumble of the bike, texture of the road, temperature of the air, and wind in my face were strangely soothing and comforting.

I am a rather typical middle-aged woman. As a public high school math teacher with three beautiful children, I have worked more than one job most of the children's lives to provide for them—tutoring, teaching night classes, even delivering food. Much of my adult life has revolved around nurturing others—my children, students, and friends. I have a big smile, light brown hair in a pixie cut, hazel eyes. and up until recently, dressed conservatively for work.

So when I first donned black leather chaps, motorcycle boots, and a helmet in 2014 to ride on the back of a motorcycle with my future second husband, I felt like a butterfly coming out of its cocoon—metamorphosizing into an entirely different yet beautiful creature ready to sprout wings and fly. It was liberating to express myself in such a different manner and to be so comfortable doing so.

I spent the next four-plus years riding on the back of my second husband's Harley. At the time, I didn't think I would ever be brave enough, strong enough, or skilled enough to ride my own bike. However, as the marriage deteriorated, I realized I might have to get my own license if I wanted to continue riding.

I met my husband in 2014 after ten years of being single and had hoped that taking my time to find the right person meant I had chosen wisely. We shared the same Christian faith, were both educators, and had similar goals in life. Unfortunately, shortly after the marriage started he began verbally and physically abusing me. Two years later, I found out that he was also deceiving me about most aspects of his life, betraying my trust in ways I never thought possible. I had hoped to save the marriage, avoid a second divorce, redeem the relationship, and keep my riding partner.

But as the hurtful aspects of the relationship continued to take their toll and I realized that I might not have the option of riding on the back of a bike much longer, I decided to face my fears and get my own endorsement. I had come to love life on the road, taking annual summer cross-country trips and visiting all forty-eight contiguous states on a bike. Although the strains of the marriage were still present on the road, I was enthralled with the sense of freedom and well-being that the bike travel gave me. I was determined not to give up biking or my summer cross-country trips, married or not.

At first, I was completely terrified even to attempt to drive a bike. I don't consider myself to be physically coordinated and had no previous motorcycle driving experience, other than a few trips on dirt bikes almost forty years earlier. So, when I decided to get my license, I took a private lesson before taking the DMV-required course at Team Oregon. The first thing I told my private instructor, Curt Erickson, was that I probably was going to either crash his bike or pass out from a panic attack. I almost hoped he would tell me I could back out of the lesson. Instead, he told me not to worry, that students "dumped" the bikes every day, and it wasn't a big deal. Sure enough, less than thirty seconds after getting on the bike, I managed to crash into the only obstacle on the large, paved parking lot—a small island with dirt and shrubs and a concrete border. I wasn't going that fast, and the bike merely shook and stalled. It seemed that it would be impossible for me to ever be somewhat competent on a bike, but by the end of the lesson, Curt had me riding in circles, stopping the bike, and even going around some cones.

My instructors at Team Oregon in McMinnville the following weekend were kind, helpful, and very encouraging. I passed the writing test with an A. But when it came time for me to take the skills test, I panicked. I was at the front of the line with eleven riders behind me, waiting and watching. The instructor stood in front of me with a clipboard. Everything I had learned that weekend went out the window. I felt so self-conscious with everyone looking at me that my heart started beating quickly, and my hands started shaking. I was supposed to demonstrate quick braking but didn't stop soon enough. When it came time to show I could go around a curve, I went outside the lines. On the cone weave, I rode over the cones or on the wrong side of them. The instructor asked at one point, "What's wrong? You were doing fine during the class." I was completely mortified and not at all surprised when I failed the test. Strangely enough, when I was getting in my car to leave after the test, relieved that at least the ordeal was over, one of my classmates came up to me and shook my hand. It was a man half my age who smiled and said, "It was an honor and a pleasure to take this class with you."

I'm still not sure why he made the comment he did, but I suspect it was because during the class my joy and passion for motorcycle riding had become evident. That weekend, as the instructor had brought up various problems and concerns related to motorcycle riding, I had enthusiastically shared stories of both mishaps and victories during my over 45,000 miles on the back of a bike crossing the country. So even though I had almost no bike driving skills, I did have a love and passion for riding that I couldn't help but express.

It was this love for riding and my determination in general that propelled me to contact Curt again and arrange for two more private lessons before re-taking the skills test the following weekend. During one of these lessons, we were practicing sharp right turns, and every single time I attempted the turn, I was terrified. I told Curt how scared I was of the turns, hoping he would offer to teach me something else, but he wouldn't let me off the hook. Instead, he said, "Well, then, it appears we need to practice the right turns a lot more."

After taking the extra private lessons, I drove to the Team Oregon skills re-test location in Beaverton and prepared to try to pass again. The head instructor there was not as encouraging as the previous instructors had been. When we were warming up before the test, I asked him a question about focusing during the turns. He replied, "If you have to ask a question like that, maybe you shouldn't be taking the test." During the actual test, my bike stopped. I tried starting it again but was unable to do so. He said, "How do you expect to pass this test if you can't even keep your bike turned on?" He came over and was also unable to start the bike, so I had to switch bikes in the middle of the test. I was sure I had failed, but I decided that I was going to give it my very best anyway. At the end, I was ecstatic to hear that, although I had gotten the worst possible score, I had actually passed the test! At that moment there was no way I could've imagined just two years later I would be traveling over 15,000 miles across the country on my own.

A huge weight had lifted off my shoulders. Instead of waiting to get my course completion card in the mail, I drove to Team Oregon headquarters in Salem on Monday to pick it up and got my motorcycle endorsement added to my license at the DMV that same day. I started the paperwork the day after that to purchase my first bike, a Honda Rebel 250. Although I only got to ride it for a few days before leaving on a six-week summer trip (still on the back of a bike), I managed to put 4,000 miles on it that fall. It was at that point I knew I needed another bike—one that would go more than sixty-five miles an hour uphill and could someday take me across the country.

I settled on a used 2018 Harley-Davidson Softail Slim just five months after getting my endorsement. The minute I sat on that bike, it was like two pieces of a puzzle fitting together. Even though I was somewhat overwhelmed at the sheer size and strength of it, I knew "the baby" was meant for me. I am rather short, but the seat was only twenty-five and a half inches off the ground, and the previous owner had put four-inch riser bars on the bike, making the machine a uniquely good fit for my small frame. Although the bike was obviously vastly heavier than my previous bike, it fit me in a similar manner. I was excited, thrilled, and a little terrified to think of the power that would be at my disposal with the new Milwaukee-Eight engine with 107 cubic inch displacement. I initially considered calling the bike the "Black Stallion" or "Black Beauty" but decided to keep with "My Baby," because I think of the bike as a natural extension of myself. I love the fact that when I pull on the throttle, "My Baby" always has more to give. He's never disappointed me.

I was diagnosed with stage-two throat cancer on November 6, 2019, less than a year after purchasing my Harley. My daughter, home from college on October 19 to be with our family pet who was dying, had asked me at the dinner table if I had a sore throat. When I said I didn't have any pain, she commented, "Well, I can see your lymph nodes from here." I went to the urgent care that weekend, my primary care provider a week later, and an ear, nose, and throat specialist on the thirtieth, who recommended a biopsy on Monday, the fourth. The specialist, aware of my teaching schedule, as I had been her daughter's math teacher, called me at the end of my school day on the sixth of November. I don't remember exactly what she said, because after I heard the word *cancer*, my ears clogged up, I had trouble hearing, and the room seemed to be spinning around me.

Fortunately, a colleague and friend of mine, Molly Hurtado, who had survived a cancer battle just months before, was in the classroom across from mine. I collapsed, crying, into her arms, shocked and in disbelief at the news. She shared some practical advice with me to help me navigate the upcoming weeks and also offered to call me that evening along with her husband, a radiologist who could shed more light on my condition. The key deciding factor regarding my prognosis, as I learned over the next several days, was going to be whether or not I had HPV-positive throat cancer or cancer associated with smoking. The former had a disease-free survival rate of eighty-five to ninety-percent over five years compared to the latter, with only a twenty-five- to forty-percent survival rate. I had never smoked a day in my life and was hopeful for the better diagnosis.

The next few weeks were a blur, as I selected the top throat cancer doctor in the area, Dr. John Holland at Oregon Health and Sciences University (OHSU), got myself fitted for a thermoplastic mask to secure myself to a table for radiation treatments, underwent surgery to remove my tonsils and biopsy my tongue, and set up my radiation and chemotherapy schedule. Although many people didn't understand my motivation, it was important to me to get the latest possible radiation treatment times so that I could continue teaching during my battle. Apparently, on average, throat cancer patients take off more than three months from work due to the pain and severity of symptoms they experience. However, I loved working with my students and felt that I would manage my pain better if I was distracted from it, rather than at home worrying about my condition.

I was at OHSU when the lab results came back, confirming I had the HPV-positive throat cancer with the higher survival rate. I called my older son, Ethan, from the waiting room of the phlebotomy department at OHSU to give him the good news. Ethan had been following my progress, researching my condition, and giving me advice about treatment options. I will never forget how much it meant to me that his voice cracked with emotion when he heard about the more positive prognosis.

The treatments were, indeed, brutal. The inside and outside of my throat were burned to the point they were raw, making it impossible for me to eat, and later, even to drink. My voice weakened and then disappeared entirely. Determined not to give up, I carried a white board with me to communicate with others, got a mic from the IT department and performing arts department to amplify my whisper so students could hear me in the classroom, and then later used a speech app on my phone along with a Bluetooth speaker to speak for me. Each day after leaving school a few minutes early to get treatment, driving to the hospital, and enduring a radiation treatment, I returned to the school campus late in the evening to grade tests, lesson plan, and return parent emails.

NOTE

Shortly after the end of my cancer treatments and before I knew whether or not they had been effective, the Oregonian and the Oregon School Boards Association each published an article about my determination to keep teaching during chemotherapy and radiation treatments. Both articles can be found on the press page of my website at kathleenterner. com/press.

At that time, I had put on over 15,000 miles driving "My Baby" and had spent several weeks of the previous summer touring ten states in the western United States with my husband, who was also riding his Harley. Once I was diagnosed, however, it was impossible for me to ride the bike anymore. I was weakened from my treatments and taking up to three different pain medications that prevented me from driving a motorcycle.

My divorce was finalized shortly after my cancer treatments ended. My cancer battle had prompted me to evaluate how I really wanted to spend the rest of my life, however limited that might be. I knew the marriage was unhealthy for both me and my children. I had stayed longer than I probably should have, because I had hoped that, somehow, the marriage could be salvaged and because I was afraid of possibly living the rest of my life alone. But the specter of death gave me the extra strength I needed to do what I had sensed for quite some time was necessary.

My fear of being alone extended to my bike. Despite whatever problems my husband and I had, he had been my riding partner on five summer cross-country trips, one each year from 2015 through 2019—the first four with me on the back and the fifth with me driving my own Harley. The summer bike trip was always the pinnacle of the year for me, and I was determined not to give that up. However, after the divorce, I had no idea whom I could ride with and did not think I had it in me to travel alone. I had only ridden my bike on my own a few times, and never for more than a few hours.

I had hoped to meet some riding partners through a variety of motorcycle groups in the area, but shortly after divorcing, the COVID-19 pandemic hit. Earlier that week, I had participated in my first HOG meeting, and that weekend I attended a barbeque at a local dealership, but from that point on, all in-person gatherings, both work and pleasure, were cancelled. I had found a few people interested in doing some longer trips, but none who had summers off, as I did as a schoolteacher.

I called my friend and neighbor, Kathleen Bufford, to commiserate about how hard it would be to find a riding partner at a time when people were distancing themselves from each other. She and her husband, Roger, have been my friends for years, and she suggested I speak with him. I explained to Roger how I really wanted to travel across the country that summer but had no idea how I could do it alone. Rather than address my fears directly, he did the best thing possible—he gave me a vision. He asked me where my older son, Ethan, lived. When I said, "Washington, DC," he responded, "Well, then, I think that's where you should ride to this summer." I replied, "But how am I going to do that on my own?" Roger's response? "Well, you have three months to figure that out."

I left that conversation with a level of hope that I had not had in a long time. My problem had gone from being impossible to simply a logistical issue. In addition, there was something compelling to me about traveling across the country to see my son. We had been separated for six months due to problems with travel during COVID. My love for him and for my other two children is one of the few things that is stronger than my deepest fears. The mother in me decided that I would do whatever it took to see him.

Delighted with my new custom seat, perfect for the road—it matches the saddlebags, moves me closer to the handlebars, and helps me sit more comfortably on the bike.

My first step was to get the bike ready for a solo ride. I ordered a sissy bar and rack for the back. Don Weber at Mr. Ed's Moto not only customized my seat so that the bike would fit my now even smaller frame, but also gave me additional confidence about embarking on my solo adventure. When setting up my appointment with him, I told him that I was going to Washington, DC, on my bike but still wasn't sure how to do it on my own. He said with a chuckle, "Well, my wife left for the dealership one day and didn't come home for two months." His wife, Debbie, had gone to the dealership to pick up a new bike and had planned to ride for a few days afterward with friends. But after the few days had passed, she called Don and said she wanted to keep going. This may sound strange, but just hearing how proud he was of his wife for her trip made me feel that it would be possible for me to do the same thing. Later, Don told me that I would learn new things about myself on my solo trip. I was skeptical about his comment, but he couldn't have been more right!

In the course of my eight-week trip, there were many milestones. I traveled over 15,000 miles through twenty-eight states and visited over a dozen national parks. On two occasions, I rode over 1,500 miles in a day and a half, earning not only two Iron Butt Association "SaddleSore" certifications but two "Bun Burners" as well. I conquered several challenging courses, including "Tail of the Dragon," "Beartooth Pass," "Million Dollar Highway," and more. I met many wonderful people, enjoyed numerous spectacular vistas, and sampled dozens of delicious meals. And by the end of the trip, I realized that Don had been right all along—I grew as a person in ways I hadn't thought possible before.

The view of the waterfall from Artist Point in Yellowstone is
particularly scenic and inspiring.

CHAPTER TWO

NEVER REALLY ALONE

Days 1–11
West Linn, Oregon, to Custer, South Dakota

Some people might wonder why I chose a Greek monastery for my first stop after leaving West Linn on my journey. Like so many places on this trip, the draw was great food, and the tip came from a fellow biker. The monastery's bakery is chock full of homemade gyros and baklava, two of my favorite foods. I traveled east on Highway 14 to Goldendale, Washington, with Grant Myers, a friend and director of the Rose City Harley Owners Group (HOG), who offered to see me off. Grant and another friend, Leo Guzman Fernandez (also a Rose City HOG member), had become regular riding partners of mine over the previous several weeks, as the three of us enjoyed longer rides with lots of curves and have an easy rapport.

TOURING TIP

To plan my trips, I get a printed map of the general geographic area where I want to travel. Then, with a highlighter, I mark the places I would like to stop. On this trip, these stops included numerous national parks, favorite hotels, scenic or challenging roads, and delicious eateries throughout the United States. After highlighting my favorite places, it is easy for me to visualize the different routes I can use to hit most or all of them. It's good to have a general route in mind but to leave the specifics up to closer to the day of travel, because I know I will want to customize based on my level of fatigue, the weather conditions, and site availability. My general plan was to go across the northern United States to the East Coast, then south to at least Tennessee, west again toward California, and then north home. I had about twenty-five things highlighted on my map and did all but a few of them on this trip. Of course, I added more highlights as I went. I also highlight the route I end up taking in a different color so I have a visual record of my trip.

The lunch at Saint John's Bakery was delicious, and the place itself was exactly what I look for on my trips—small, unassuming, a little quirky, and full of great food. The nuns there make the beef gyros with tender, juicy meat fresh to order each day. They also offer coffee, homemade jam, savory pastries, and desserts. I enjoyed the food so much I decided to get a spanakopita (made with crispy layers of phyllo dough and spinach and feta cheese filling) and some baklava to go.

After eating, Grant and I walked out to our bikes. It seemed like the perfect time to leave—the sun was shining, the temperature was mild, the roads were clear, and there was a lot of light left in the day. However, my feelings were somewhat mixed. I felt a heightened sense of awareness about my surroundings as the minute of departure neared—a combination of excitement as well as trepidation. Almost like heading toward the top of a roller coaster ride, knowing you are going to love the drop down the other side but still feeling somewhat apprehensive about the suddenness of it all.

The moment seemed rather significant to me—after all, I was leaving on an eight-week trip completely on my own without having done even a two-day solo trip before. I expected a little pep talk like "You've got this" or "Have a great trip." In retrospect, though, Grant did something even more helpful—he conveyed confidence in me by simply saying, "I'd better head back," and then leaving. After he turned west toward home, I looked at my bike loaded up with my two travel bags and thought, "Oh no, what have I done?"

The day had gotten off to a rocky start. I live at the bottom of a steep driveway on a busy city street. It is always a challenge to give the bike enough throttle to make it up the hill but not so much that I overshoot the driveway and get run over by cross traffic. That morning, with my bike loaded up, I had given it more throttle than usual and ended up going two feet out into the street, just narrowly missing a passing speeding car, so I was already a little rattled before I had really started. Then at the bakery other doubts came to my mind: "What if I drop the bike, get lost, or have mechanical trouble?" All of these things did end up happening on the trip. But I think my biggest fear was, "How am I going to handle being alone for two months?"

After my divorce in February, I had been praying for months for a summer riding partner, without success. I went on many group rides and thoroughly enjoyed the camaraderie I shared with my new friends over meals afterward. Because I love to ride so much, I would often extend the ride on my own. I had started to learn that there were some uniquely wonderful aspects to riding alone—I could go as slow or fast as I chose, pull over when I wanted, eat where I wanted, and totally immerse myself in the ride. Group rides provided great opportunities to build friendships, but I found my solo rides were the best way to feed my soul.

Making the decision to do my eight-week, cross-country trip on my own was not insignificant to me. For years, I had struggled with a visceral fear of being alone. This fear was so pronounced that it was part of my reason for staying in a marriage fraught with lies and betrayals. I was miserable in the marriage but sure that I would be more miserable alone. I felt trapped, with nowhere to go. My oldest child, Ethan, concerned for my emotional well-being, had taken me out for dinner alone the previous fall and asked how I was doing. I decided to be honest with him. I looked him right in the eye and said, "Sometimes I wish I just didn't have to wake up in the morning."

Fortunately, I was able to do what I needed to do and end the marriage shortly thereafter, paving the way for a much healthier and happier future. But I had always had my husband with me on my cross-country trips. Regardless of whatever problems we had, I knew if I had an issue with my bike there would be someone there to help me with it.

Once I made the decision to go solo, I shifted from being afraid of being alone to planning for being alone. The practical issues were rather straightforward. I had gotten the good news on April 22 that my cancer was in remission, so I was cleared to go from a health standpoint. I made sure I had the necessary automobile club coverage, got my bike serviced, and put on new tires. My friend, Kathy Nesper, was concerned about the risks to me riding alone, so we arranged for me to share my mobile phone map so she could track my location at all times. I also agreed to text her at the end of each day that I was safely "in for the night." I knew if I was injured on the side of the road, she would be able to call for help, even if I couldn't.

The biggest issue for me, though, was wondering how I would feel about seeing so many beautiful places and eating so much delicious food but having no one to share the experience with in the moment. I also wasn't sure how I would feel alone in a hotel room night after night. I did plan ahead for this to some extent. After my cancer treatments were over and my divorce finalized, I had started a daily journal to help me have a more positive outlook. Each day I wrote out a whole page of "I am grateful for . . ." statements, and I found that I always had more positive things to think about than I originally realized. This practice had helped me to see life through a lens of gratitude, and now I added arrangements to check in with my children regularly while on the road. I also decided to post regular updates to my Facebook account during my trip, so that I could share my journey with friends, even if they weren't with me in person.

But there was still so much I didn't know about how I would handle the solitude. A big turning point for me was a growing realization about how I could draw on my personal faith for strength in times of difficulty. As a Christian, I had known about all three parts of the Trinity for years—God the Father, Jesus the Son, and the Holy Spirit. But I had only a vague understanding of the Holy Spirit. After my divorce in February, I had joined two women's Bible studies. Interestingly enough, I ended up learning through my connection with each that the Holy Spirit lives within me and is in a very real sense both my friend and my helper. The Holy Spirit speaks to me, prays for me, and teaches me. Learning this made the Spirit's presence seem more real to me. I had been asking for a riding partner for months but hadn't realized I already had one! I understand that not everyone shares the same faith, but I think we all find a greater sense of strength and inner well-being when we relate our lives to something bigger than just ourselves.

I became more acutely aware that I am never really alone. How freeing! It was such a relief to go from having a truly primeval fear of being alone to a growing sense of assurance that I had all the companionship I really needed within me all along. I became more and more convinced that God would not only provide me with company but also help me to have positive interactions with others I met on the trip.

Of course, it is one thing to have this "aha moment" in a Bible study and an entirely different thing to test it by planning a two-month solo trip!

My first day on the road, Wednesday, July 1, was reassuring. I quickly learned that my trip would be full of positive, interesting, and meaningful conversations with people from all walks of life. After leaving Grant at the bakery, I headed north to the Country Mercantile in Pasco, Washington—another food stop. The store was loaded with row after row of homemade chocolates, candies, fudge, and ice cream, as well as fresh fruit. While waiting for a scoop of ice cream, I asked the group ordering before me to describe the flavors. Since recovering from my cancer treatments just a few months before, I had yet to regain all of my sense of taste, so I was curious to hear from them how good the ice cream was. One of the members of the group, a doctor, ended up sitting down at a picnic table with me later while I ate my ice cream. Over the course of fifteen minutes, he asked about my cancer, my career as a teacher during the pandemic, and my trip. He discussed his own career choices and life. He was surprisingly frank with his feelings and interested in how I had been emotionally impacted by the events of the previous several months. It was surreal and at the same time reassuring to be discussing such meaningful topics with someone I had just met.

While walking to my bike afterward, a trucker, who was parked in the store's large parking lot, introduced himself. He explained that he loved to ride and that one day he hoped to put his bike on his truck so he could ride it during stops. He talked about his work, as well as his concern that he might not make it home to his family in Chicago in time to spend the weekend with them. I was struck by how forthright and open this long-haul trucker was and could understand his emotions. I was longing to see my own son on the East Coast and eager to be there with him. I stopped my bike again just a few miles away at the Fiesta Foods in town to get some snacks to eat on the road. While I was in the parking lot there, another guy said he had the same goggles that I had. He shared about his passion for helping families in crisis and showed me some of his Facebook posts.

I was a little unnerved by how fervent he was about his projects but reassured myself that I could hop on the bike at any time to leave. Later, when I checked into my hotel, another man recounted his experience with a high-speed motorcycle chase in his youth and his growing maturity since then. I could relate to both aspects of his story—the desire for speed on the bike as well as the realization of the importance of riding safely.

Needless to say, by the time I got to my hotel room, I felt a strengthening sense of encouragement that my trip would not be filled with loneliness, but rather with healthy times of reflection as well as interesting and vastly different conversations with people I might not normally meet.

The next day I headed north to Bonners Ferry and a favorite hotel there, run by a young couple. When I checked in, I realized that the wife was not at the desk. When asked, the new manager explained that the owner's wife had died unexpectedly from colon cancer since the time I had seen her the previous summer. It was a sobering reminder to me of the importance of living life to the fullest while I am still able. That night, the husband started a bonfire for his hotel guests, and I had the opportunity to hear about his situation, as well as to share stories and trip ideas with several other bikers who were also spending the night.

The time around the fire was confidence building for me. I had noticed the group of men congregating there when I came back from dinner. Being a single woman traveling alone, I was not sure how they would respond to me joining the conversation. But the night was mild, the fire looked inviting, and I was interested in building rapport with others on the road. I was pleased to find that I was welcomed into the group. The men did seem somewhat surprised that I was planning on traveling such long distances on my own, but they were extremely friendly and supportive.

I headed east to Glacier National Park on Friday. After checking in at my hotel in Kalispell, I was able to ride the first fourteen or so miles of the Going-to-the-Sun Road. Because the roads accumulate up to eighty feet of snow during winter, it takes months for them to be cleared. Although the majority of the road was still closed to through traffic, I was fortunate to be able to ride along the ten-mile stretch of Lake McDonald. The temperature was in the mid-70s, the lake waters were blue and smooth, and the lush trees provided rich shade canopies. I was excited to be in the park, even though I couldn't go through to the east entrance.

Mesmerized by the many dazzling shades of green in the meadows and hills between Philipsburg and Anaconda, Montana

The following day, I took backroads through Philipsburg and Anaconda on my way to Butte, Montana. The vistas were remarkable—strikingly bold shades of yellow and green fields surrounded by white and gray mountain peaks. These colorful fields and mountain views made taking the backroads especially rewarding. My GPS was determined to send me back to Interstate 90, but I persisted in staying off the beaten path, knowing that my paper map could get me where I needed to go.

TOURING TIP

While the map app on my phone is invaluable for guiding me from destination to destination, I have learned that it is not infallible. I have had the app direct me to take roads that are closed or do not exist or fail to inform me of roads that are available, even when I am stopped right in front of them. In other cases, such as this time in Montana, the app was directing me over a hundred miles out of my way, when a shorter route was available. I had taken backroads through Philipsburg and Anaconda on my way to lodging in Butte, but the app kept trying to direct me back the way I had come up Highway 1 to Drummond and down Interstate 90 to Butte. As a result of these GPS challenges, I always carry paper maps with me for all of the places I will visit. I am an AAA member and have access to unlimited maps. Since I usually travel across the country and back and like to have the flexibility to change plans, I typically get two United States maps, one each of the regional maps (for instance the southeast states), and then several of the state maps for states I am pretty certain I would like to spend extra time in.

While in Butte, I made reservations for the next two nights at Chico Hot Springs in Pray, Montana. I love this historic resort because it is close to Yellowstone National Park, offers very reasonable room rates, sports a natural hot springs pool, and has a fine dining room with excellent steaks and desserts.

I had called a few times to see if they had any last-minute openings for lodging. I tend to book close to my date of arrival, as so many unexpected events can make an exact arrival date on a motorcycle hard to predict. The reservation clerk at this point was familiar with the fact that I was traveling on a motorcycle and also that I was traveling alone. When I booked the reservations, she told me she would give me a ten-percent discount because she thought the idea of a woman traveling alone on a bike was "bad ass." Her comment warmed my heart as a middle-aged mom of three grown children and gave me more confidence that the solo trip was going to end up being a grand adventure.

Taking Montana backroads from Kalispell to Butte was time well spent.

After checking into the hotel, I rode the bike to Yellowstone and visited my favorite spot in the park, Artist Point. Artist Point is an overlook on the edge of a cliff on the south rim of the Grand Canyon of the Yellowstone, with a view of the 308-foot lower falls of the Yellowstone River. The falls are displayed in a deep, V-shaped canyon made of vivid orange rocks, and they spew from 5,000 to 60,000 gallons of water every second. I have always found waterfalls to be inspiring and therapeutic. There is something in them that speaks to me of strength, hope, and serenity. The previous summer, I had visited this very spot during an extremely trying time in my failing marriage. That time at the overlook I felt a few rare moments of peace. I was so happy to be back there now under better terms, free of the strains of a painful relationship and feeling the beginning groundswells of gratitude, hope, and optimism.

A wide, covered porch surrounded by blooming flowers at Chico Hot
Springs provides the perfect place to read a book
and relax after a day of riding.

After taking several pictures of the waterfalls and soaking
up their majesty, I headed back to the bike to visit the Norris
Geyser Basin. The basin is beautiful in a very different
manner than the waterfalls—milky blue sections of hot water,
surrounded by a stark white, gray, and steaming landscape.
The raised pathway there makes it possible to see this vibrant,
dynamic natural wonder up close.

The ride leaving the park going north to Chico Hot
Springs was more invigorating than the driving in the park,
as there was less traffic, the speed limit was higher, and the
roads were in better condition. I had purposely made my
dinner reservation late and arrived in plenty of time to enjoy
reading a book on the flower-covered porch and swimming in
the resort's natural hot springs swimming pool before eating
in the main dining room. While swimming in the hot springs,
I had a delightful conversation with a mother of four young
children, two of whom were twins. The fact that I am also

the mother of boy-girl twins gave us an instant rapport. It was rewarding to see the love between her and her family and to chat mom to mom.

The raised pathway at Norris Geyser Basin allows visitors to have an up-close encounter with the milky blue-colored hot springs and steaming landscape—the hottest, oldest, and most dynamic of Yellowstone's thermal areas.

For dinner that night I enjoyed the gorgonzola filet mignon—an eight ounce Angus beef hand rubbed with toasted fennel, sea salt, pepper and coriander and served with a port reduction and gorgonzola crumbles. Since the injuries sustained to my throat during cancer treatments still made it difficult for me to swallow steak, I ordered extra port reduction, both to help me eat and also because it tasted so delicious. I also thoroughly enjoyed the resort's homemade gratin of local potatoes topped with gruyere and gorgonzola, followed by a fresh, homemade berry cobbler. Gruyere is one of my favorite cheeses, partially because of the taste and also because it reminds me of eating cheese fondue with my grandmother in Switzerland. It was easy to sleep that night, full of happy memories and good food and nestled in my rustic, well-appointed room at the resort.

The following day I visited Old Faithful and got to see the park's buffalo. On this day, I decided to just breathe in the park, be attentive to my surroundings, and live in the moment. I took no pictures in the park, other than one video while Old Faithful was erupting. I loved sitting in the shade on the grass and watching the majestic plume of water rocket up into the sky. I find it amazing and inspiring that the water gushes up with such regularity. It was almost surreal, talking with other tourists about when the next "scheduled" eruption was due, as if the exact time the pressure from the trapped steam would be released was something that should be printed up on a program for the day. That evening I took my time driving through the park back to the north entrance, taking in the buffalo herds and lush green meadows.

For months I had been anticipating Tuesday's ride leaving the park via Beartooth Pass. I left Pray, re-entered Yellowstone, and this time skirted the north end of the park, heading toward the northeast entrance. While still in the park, I had the unexpected pleasure of seeing a grizzly bear and then, less than two minutes later, watching a large male buffalo chase a small black bear! I was so astounded by the site of the buffalo charging the bear that I wondered if I'd imagined it and asked a fellow park visitor if she had seen the same thing. She laughed, confirmed the sighting, and then asked me about my trip and if I was traveling alone. I explained that I had embarked on cross-country motorcycle trips the previous five summers with my husband, had divorced just a few months earlier, and had decided I didn't want to give up my summer adventure, even if it meant traveling on my own. She was intrigued, supportive, and affirming, even joking, "How cool! I feel like I'm cooler just for having met you."

Feeling on top of the world on Beartooth Pass

The road from Beartooth Pass to Red Lodge, Montana, had been on my top five must-do routes every summer since I started motorcycling six years before, and after admiring the wildlife, I had the privilege of riding it again. (The previous summer had been the first time I had ridden it on my own bike.) The route is particularly thrilling, because it is in great condition and includes an almost endless supply of tight turns and figure eights. Leaning into the curves and balancing the bike through all the twists and bends in the road is challenging and invigorating. The ride is picturesque as well. As the elevation rises, the temperature drops and snow appears on the side of the road, even in the middle of summer. Beautiful, snow-capped mountain peaks materialize around every twist and turn, providing a visually stunning experience that stands in marked contrast to the warm, lush green meadows in the park below. This year there was a rather significant side wind blowing, making the driving much more technically challenging than usual. It was still an absolute delight to ride—the equivalent of enjoying an excellent dessert, absolutely delicious and satisfying.

One of many glorious hairpin turns on Beartooth Pass from
Yellowstone National Park to Red Lodge, Montana

When I arrived at my hotel in Red Lodge, I met an elderly
couple traveling in their three-wheeled vehicle. They provided
me with my first opportunity for turning what could be
a negative interaction into a positive one. The couple had
been surprised to hear about my situation, and the wife said,
"What are you doing traveling alone?" By that point I had
developed enough confidence about my decision that I was
able to answer her question with, "Having the adventure of
a lifetime." She paused for a moment, grinned, and then said,
"Good for you!" It was freeing and exhilarating to realize, in
that moment, that I was happy to be traveling alone, without
relying on, or seeking, another's approval.

That night I dined at one of my favorite Italian restaurants
in the country, Piccola Cucina. The food is authentic Italian,
and the atmosphere is festive and light. While I waited outside
next to my motorcycle for my table to become available, I met
another woman traveler, also from Oregon. She was intrigued
by the fact I was traveling alone on my bike and wanted to

know more about my background. After I explained about my recent divorce and determination to ride with or without a partner, she made the remark, "You know what's going to happen on this trip, don't you? You're going to meet your next husband." I considered her comment for a minute and responded with a smile, "I'm not sure I actually want another one." What a transformation I was already making in my life!

On several occasions during dinner, the hostess turned up the music and invited guests to dance. The atmosphere was very much that of a party, with the chefs throwing oil on the grill so that flames could be seen leaping up through the kitchen window while the music pulsed. I decided to take part in the festivities and danced to the music with one of the waiters. Later in the evening, when the music was turned up again, a conga line snaked its way past my table, and I decided to join it. I may have been sitting on my own at the table, but I did not feel at all alone in the restaurant.

The next day I headed to one of my favorite motels in the country, the Rocket Motel in Custer, South Dakota, not far from Sturgis. The motel is a home away from home for me and is one of the few places I always spend more than one night. The couple who run it, Don and Brenda Herren, are friendly and helpful. Don is a former motorcyclist himself, has designated motorcycle parking, and provides rags for washing bikes. The rooms are reasonably priced, clean, and cheerful, with a retro-style décor that includes black and white tiles, clean white bedspreads, colorful accents, and red rotary phones that actually work. Best yet, the motel provides the perfect home base for exploring some of the best motorcycle terrain in the country—Custer State Park and the Black Hills. Don and Brenda remembered me from years past and took the time to ask me about my divorce and my cancer battle.

My three full days in Custer were delightful and restorative, with the Rocket Motel providing a familiar and comfortable launching pad for numerous adventures. The first day there I was thrilled to tackle Needles Highway in Custer State Park.

The road is full of twists and turns, challenging corners, and one curve that seems to go on forever. The scenery is distinctive: granite pillars, towers, and spires. I had seen Rocky Mountain goats from that road in the past. It was a pleasure to lean into the curves, focus on the technical aspect of the ride, and also look up at the tall rock towers. That same day I also explored the Wildlife Loop. This year there were no close encounters with wildlife, but I still enjoyed the long, meandering road through meadows and trees.

One of the things I love about riding in the Black Hills is the variety of landscapes. Having appreciated the rock spires of Needles and the bucolic meadows and rugged hills of the Wildlife Loop, I was looking forward to yet another adventure on my second full day of riding when I travelled on Iron Mountain Road. This road, which connects Custer State Park and Mount Rushmore National Memorial, boasts three stone tunnels that frame the massive granite sculptures. It's such a joy to ride on a twisty road with great overlooks and also be treated to a unique view of a spectacular national treasure.

What a treat—a view of Mount Rushmore through this tunnel on Iron Mountain Road in Custer State Park

The third day of riding was more low-key, including a visit to the Harley-Davidson dealership in Sturgis and some brief pit stops at overlooks for Bridal Veil Falls and Spearfish Falls.

A close-up of the view of George Washington, Thomas Jefferson, Abraham Lincoln, and Theodore Roosevelt from the other side of the tunnel

The last night in Custer, as I contemplated the riding challenges I would be taking on over the next several days, I realized that I had more company and human contact on the trip than I ever thought possible. In addition to a developing awareness of God's presence in my life, my daily conversations with friends or my children, the nightly safety check-ins via text, and frequent conversations with fellow travelers, I was also blessed with the support and encouragement of many friends on Facebook.

Each day after I posted pictures and descriptions of my rides, my friends would respond with encouraging and affirming comments, cheering me on, and I felt as if they were on the ride with me. Molly Hurtado, my fellow math teacher, pronounced, "You are bad ass!!" Mark Silva, a friend from Rose City HOG, faithfully responded every day with positive comments like, "Awesome! Keep it up! Just Ride." Tony

Clawson, another riding companion, declared, "You're a Rock Star. Love keeping track of your travel!! What a blessing!!" Rod Meyer, Oregon regional director for Black Sheep Harley-Davidsons for Christ, told me, "We are all following you as if we were there." Sally Harlow, another Black Sheep member, exclaimed, "I'm totally living vicariously through your pictures." Trace Fleming, a rider I had met through posting about my trip, congratulated me: "Bravo on taming that angry turn."

While I had been traveling for only eleven days, I feel that I had already experienced a life-changing, radically freeing sense of awareness that I was never really alone.

Feeling a sense of rebirth and hope while soaking
in the waters of Niagara Falls under a rainbow

CHAPTER THREE

STRONGER THAN I REALIZE

Days 12–14
Custer, South Dakota, to Niagara Falls, New York

About six weeks before leaving on my solo trip, on a group ride to Klickitat, Washington, and Mount Hood, Oregon, I overheard my friend, Jenni Cramer, talking about her "Iron Butt" ride. My ears perked up when I heard "1,000 miles." That couldn't be in one day, could it? Intrigued, I asked about her accomplishment, and she introduced me to the Iron Butt Association (IBA) and their endurance rides. Motorcyclists who provide detailed documentation to the IBA of rides of at least 1,000 miles in under twenty-four hours can receive an "Iron Butt" certification. From the moment I heard that, I was hooked!

It's hard to describe what it feels like to hear about an opportunity and just know it's something you were meant to do. It was the same feeling as the moment I realized that I was meant to be a high school math teacher. As an adult, I had gone back to college to get my teaching credential, and as part of my coursework, I had observed a more senior teacher in her high school algebra class. She was strong, capable, effective, and compassionate with her students. I could tell they knew she cared deeply about them and that she was helping them achieve to the very best of their abilities. At that moment, a light went on in my head. I went from being somewhat unsure about what kind of teacher I would be to knowing with certainty I was meant to be just like her.

For me, riding a motorcycle has been a similar experience, although it is a pastime I started later in life, I feel it is something I was born to do. Within a few weeks of getting on the back of a bike for the first time as an adult, I was headed off on a seven-day road trip as a passenger with my future second husband. Just a little over a year later, we departed for a seven-week, cross-country trip from Oregon to Maine and back, with him driving us both on his Harley. Then just four years after that I got my own license and bike, opening up an even bigger world of opportunities for me. From 2014, when I first started riding on the back of a bike to the end of this solo trip, I rode over 100,000 miles during day and night, in snow and hail, amid thunder and lightning, and through intense heat and bitter cold. Yet I can't remember a single time when I ever felt like I had ridden too much or traveled too many miles.

There had been many occasions when I had ridden several hundred miles in one day but none where I came close to 1,000. On one particular occasion in the fall of 2018, shortly after getting my first bike, I decided I wanted to ride to Medford, Oregon, and back in one day, a round trip of 536 miles, so that I could have an In-N-Out burger for lunch. On many occasions I have driven 200 to 400 miles roundtrip to the coast or to Central Oregon within twenty-four hours. The summer before this trip, I rode through ten states on my Harley and often went several hundred miles in one day. But there was something compelling and irresistible to me about the idea of going 1,000 miles in twenty-four hours and being "Iron Butt" certified. I decided that my solo cross-country trip would provide the perfect opportunity for me to attempt the challenge.

Before leaving on my trip, I researched ride requirements, printed out documents I would need to submit to the IBA, and became a member of the Iron Butt discussion forum so I could get more information. I wasn't sure where I would attempt my ride, but I wanted to be ready for whenever and wherever the opportunity presented itself. I looked at my travel map and identified a few long stretches of interstate that might make good candidates. I tentatively planned to begin from Custer, South Dakota, because I knew I would be well rested after staying at the Rocket Motel. I hadn't planned for any essential overnight stops between South Dakota and the East Coast, so starting the ride from South Dakota would allow me to try the challenge without missing any of my favorite destinations. There was an added motive to make good mileage toward the East Coast early on in my journey: I was anxious to see my older son in Washington, DC, whom I missed terribly after having been separated for six long months due to COVID-19 travel restrictions.

Touring Tip

The IBA Forum is an excellent place to ask questions about the challenges and requirements of completing an IBA-certified ride. The members are extremely helpful and encouraging. Eric Vaillancourt, who has completed several IBA-certified rides, provided me with many helpful tips, such as numbering my gas receipts, different kinds of ear plugs to consider, and ways to stay hydrated.

My attempt to complete the Iron Butt challenge began rather inauspiciously at 10 AM in Custer, South Dakota, on a Sunday. I am much more of a night person than a morning person and decided not to leave too early, knowing I would be able to ride longer if I got a good night's sleep. Within two miles of leaving the first gas station, I realized I had left one of my luggage compartments unzipped, so I had to pull over and zip up the bag. Then I got stuck behind an RV and a slow-moving truck carrying hay. I had known that it might be smarter to start out closer to the interstate but figured I had enough time to travel the forty-five miles from Custer through the countryside to get there. Although I was a little apprehensive at first about the delays so early in my endurance ride, I reassured myself that I could make up for the lost time later and decided to just relax and enjoy the ride through the country.

I stopped for gas in Rapid City, South Dakota, at the entrance to Interstate 90, not because I actually needed gas or to take a break, but because the IBA asks riders who are attempting the Iron Butt Challenge to get a gas receipt at any "turning point" in their trip. The IBA counts the mileage for their endurance rides by plotting the shortest distance between the beginning and ending points of the trip and needs proof regarding any turns in the route. I headed east on Interstate 90 for 130 miles and stopped for gas again in Murdo, South Dakota. As with most of my stops, I had a protein drink to stay hydrated and keep my energy level high. After traveling another 139 miles to Mitchell, South Dakota, I had a surprising revelation—I was absolutely loving the sense of freedom I felt from riding just for the sake of riding. There were no planned stops for food or sightseeing. No decisions about what back road was the best route. Just several hundred miles of glorious freeway beckoning me east. I was full of energy and ready to go much farther.

While ordering a Burrito Supreme at a Taco Bell at a service station in Mitchell, I had a crazy thought—what if instead of stopping at 1,000 miles in Saint Joseph, Michigan, I went another 500 and made it all the way to Niagara Falls? I had picked St. Joseph as a stopping point because it was a little over 1,000 miles east of Custer, with nothing but interstate travel after Rapid City. But there was nothing in particular I

wanted to do in St. Joseph and a lot I wanted to see at Niagara
Falls. I remembered that the IBA had a "Bun Burner" award
for certified rides of at least 1,500 miles in less than thirty-six
hours. I had encountered strong cross winds earlier in the day
but no other weather problems since then. After I confirmed
that there were no weather issues that might hinder my travel
past St. Joseph, I resolved to try to make it to Niagara, New
York, by the end of the following day.

Before leaving on my endurance ride, I had assumed the
biggest challenge I'd be facing would be fatigue; I couldn't
have imagined that it would turn out to be finding gas. The
first hint of trouble came when I was over a hundred miles
east of Mitchell. I knew I was not travelling through densely
populated areas, and since I only had a five-gallon gas tank,
I wanted to stop for gas sooner rather than later. But when
I saw a billboard advertising gas just west of Worthington,
Minnesota, and pulled over, the gas station was closed. When
I pulled over a few miles later at the Cenex in Worthington, I
almost couldn't get gas there either. It was only 6 PM, but they
were closing early, and the only way to get gas from the pump
was by paying the teller inside. If I had been five minutes later,
I would have been out of luck. Fortunately, I did find gas 130
miles later in Albert Lea, Minnesota, and again another 130
miles east in Onalaska, Wisconsin.

By that point, I was starting to worry about my next stops.
It was after 10 PM when I left Onalaska, and I knew that it
would be much harder to find service stations that were open
overnight. I was still feeling fairly unsettled by my close call
earlier in the evening, realizing I had nearly had to abort the
ride due to lack of gas. I briefly texted and messaged a few
friends, asking them to pray that I would be able to find gas
after midnight as I continued east on Interstate 90. I was
very relieved when I saw a neon sign for a twenty-four-hour
Citgo station less than 150 miles later in Madison, Wisconsin.
After exiting the freeway, turning onto a side road, and
driving up a steep hill, I was confronted with a frustrating

contradiction—a closed gas station next to a neon sign loudly advertising "24-hour" gas.

Determined not to give up, I got back on the interstate and tried another exit a few miles down the road. A middle-aged man stopped at the light next to me. I got his attention and asked if he knew where I could get gas. He answered that he believed there was gas down the side road to my right. I thanked him and headed that way, only to find that the road was under construction and I had to drive over a section of wet concrete, followed by a construction worker a short distance later telling me that gas station was also closed. It was now almost 1 AM, and the news was disheartening. I had already traveled about 140 miles since last gassing up and was now leaving the last major city before Chicago, another 145 miles away. I knew that my five-gallon tank would run out of gas long before I could reach the Windy City.

To be honest, I am typically a rather determined person, but at that moment I felt somewhat defeated. I pulled my bike into the median opposite the wet concrete, and with the freeway onramp in sight, leaned over my handlebars and shed a few tears. It was such a helpless feeling to need gas, to be told that gas was available, and to go up a steep hill or over wet concrete to find it, only to discover, for whatever reason, that there was none. The fact the ride was being timed added even more to my stress level.

I let myself cry for less than a minute. And then I took a few deep breaths and evaluated my options. I was on my own and it was up to me to figure out my next steps. I had enough gas to make it to a hotel for the night but didn't want to give up that easily. Ever since I was a little girl, my mother had told me, "Kathleen, if you want something badly enough and put your mind to it, you can accomplish it."

Starting in childhood, I internalized her message, her words becoming part of how I saw myself as a person.

Of course, as I had since discovered, sometimes no matter how badly we want something, God has other plans for us. The failure of my second marriage made this perfectly clear. Still, I am grateful for my mother's words, because they helped me learn that I would rather try to succeed and fail than to give up without even trying. Perhaps because of this perspective, I am particularly moved by Theodore Roosevelt's comments on the subject:

> *It is not the critic who counts; not the man who points out how the strong man stumbles, or where the doer of deeds could have done them better. The credit belongs to the man who is actually in the arena, whose face is marred by dust and sweat and blood; who strives valiantly; who errs, who comes short again and again, because there is no effort without error and shortcoming; but who does actually strive to do the deeds; who knows great enthusiasms, the great devotions; who spends himself in a worthy cause; who at the best knows in the end the triumph of high achievement, and who at the worst, if he fails, at least fails while daring greatly, so that his place shall never be with those cold and timid souls who neither know victory nor defeat.*
>
> *—Theodore Roosevelt*

These words paint a vivid picture of the courage and valor required to throw ourselves wholeheartedly into an endeavor, whether or not the outcome is what we yearn for. I sometimes write this quote on the extra white board in my classroom, hoping to encourage and inspire my students not to give up when they face difficulties.

After evaluating my options—pulling over at a hotel or continuing on in search of gas—I decided I would rather keep looking for gas and run out than give up my search. I knew that I had AAA road service and could call for roadside assistance if necessary. So I wiped the wet concrete off my bike, took a few more deep breaths, sat up straight, gripped my handlebars with determination, and headed for the freeway on-ramp. A few miles later, in Cottage Grove, I found gas at the Road Ranger station and gratefully filled up my bike.

I had assumed that as I approached Chicago my gas woes would be over. What I hadn't expected was that the expressway would lack clearly marked signs for exits with gas. I was travelling through the heart of Chicago at 2:30 in the morning with semis bearing down on me, unable to see signs of fuel anywhere. There were no shoulders and nowhere to pull over and use my phone to check for nearby gas. All of the exits were poorly lit, and I wasn't comfortable exiting into the unknown territory of urban Chicago to find out what was off the expressway. My mind started to create worst-case scenarios as the tank inched closer to empty with every passing mile. What would happen to me, I wondered, if I ran out of gas on the expressway, had nowhere to pull over, and got run over by a speeding semi unable to see me stranded in the roadway? Fortunately, at three o'clock in the morning, I finally saw a sliver of a Shell gas station sign near an exit and managed to make the turn in time. I felt like kissing the gas station attendant when I saw her!

As I left Chicago, I knew I had enough gas to make it to my pit-stop in St. Joseph for the "night." I would be arriving around 6 AM to crash for a few hours before continuing down the interstate in my pursuit of 1,500 miles. Unbeknownst to me, there was one more obstacle I would face before I could stop—tollbooths.

Before leaving Oregon, I had called my local AAA office to inquire about getting a tollbooth pass for the toll roads I would encounter after leaving the western states. From previous summer travels with my husband, I knew that tollbooths— stations where fees are collected for traveling on particular routes—were common in the Midwest and East and that they could be particularly unpleasant for motorcyclists.

I had hoped to save time and make my travel easier by using a prepaid pass that would allow me to travel through express lanes without stopping at the booths. Because so many cars stop at the booths in the lanes designated for travelers without a pass, there is often oil, a slick spot, or debris on the pavement, presenting a safety hazard when on a bike. In addition, it is time consuming and awkward to stop the bike, turn off the bike, take off your gloves, get your credit card out, put the card away, put the gloves back on, re-start the bike, and continue on your way. Unfortunately, the AAA representative told me I couldn't buy a toll pass in advance. He assured me that it wasn't necessary because all of the booths now had the ability to read my license plate and send me a bill. He also said I could get a pass at most of the gas stations in the Midwest. However, I had asked for a toll pass at every stop on my endurance ride, and not a single gas station had them for sale.

After leaving the Shell station in Chicago, I made it through a couple toll booths without incident, as there was, indeed, a lane designated for motorists who wished to have their license plates scanned and to be charged later. Unfortunately, I soon came to a toll station that required travelers without a pre-paid card to pay at a booth. But the booth wouldn't accept my credit card, and there was no attendant on duty at four o'clock in the morning. Finally, I managed to get through by pushing a help button and speaking to someone remotely. A few miles down the road, I was again required to stop, and that time I was not so lucky. The booth was unattended, wouldn't take my cash or card, and no one responded to the "help" button. So, after waiting ten or fifteen minutes with no reply, I made the decision to drive around the bars. I found out the next day, from an attendant at a similar booth, that sometimes the sensors in the road lack the sensitivity to detect motorcyclists. She assured me I had done the right thing by driving around.

I was relieved to arrive in St. Joseph at 6 AM to get my last gas for the night and make a brief stop at the Econo Lodge to sleep for a few hours. Although I had completed the 1,000-mile "SaddleSore" portion of my ride, I was still determined to make it to Niagara Falls in time to earn the "Bun Burner 1500" award as well, so I checked out just before noon to start the last 500 miles of my ride. Fortunately, the ride that day traveling east on Interstate 80 was completely uneventful. All but one of the gas stations I stopped at were open, and I felt more and more relaxed the closer I got to New York.

I felt almost indescribable elation approaching Niagara Falls around nine o'clock in the evening on Monday after having left Custer, South Dakota, only the morning before. I was so proud of myself for persevering through so many challenges—strong cross winds, closed gas stations, road construction, wet concrete, and unresponsive toll booths. I had traveled through nine states, three time zones, and over 1,500 miles in less than thirty-four hours on my own, just two years after getting my motorcycle endorsement. I was excited to see Niagara Falls again and to be so close to my son in Washington, DC. The approach to Niagara Falls took me through Buffalo and over the river just as the sun was setting. The sky was purple and pink above the blue water, and I remember thinking that I didn't know life could be so full of joy.

Jubilant at Niagara Falls after completing two certified Iron Butt Association endurance rides

When I checked into my hotel around 10 PM, I was surprised to find that the falls were within walking distance. As with almost all my stops, I had simply picked the least expensive lodging in town, and I didn't have any idea that the hotel was so ideally situated. The desk clerk told me that the falls were lit up at night, so after briefly dropping off my bags and changing into flip-flops, I took the short walk to them. What a delight! The falls were lit up in red, white, and blue and were simply magnificent. I got some amazing pictures and videos and didn't think it would be possible to experience anything better the next day. After all, what could be more amazing than Niagara lit up at night?

A view to revel in—stunning Niagara Falls
from the *Maiden of the Mist* boat tour

I slept in the next day and decided to take the day off from riding. I wanted to fully explore Niagara Falls and could walk to everything I wanted to see. So, after mailing my gas station receipts and ride forms to the Iron Butt Association, I grabbed a quick lunch and headed to the falls. One of my riding friends had reminded me of the *Maiden of the Mist* boat tour. I had been on the tour with my husband four years earlier during one of our summer motorcycle trips but made the mistake of taking so many pictures I didn't really "drink in" the splendor of the falls. This time I got a few quick shots but spent almost all of the tour fully absorbing the beauty around me.

I had been given a rain poncho to use on the boat but decided not to use it, so that I could not only see and hear the falls but feel the water from them as well. It was very hot outside, and the cold water felt so refreshing! After the boat tour, I went on the Cave of the Winds tour that included a walkway right under a portion of the falls. Because of the COVID-19 pandemic, the tour was limited to a few people at a time, so I had several moments on my own to walk under the falls, lift my head up into the water, and let it cascade over me. Just at that moment, a double rainbow appeared over the falls.

I have always seen rainbows in the biblical sense: as a sign of hope. The whole cross-country solo trip was a celebration of life after so recently surviving both throat cancer and a divorce. Standing there with the water running down all over me and the rainbows above me, I felt truly reborn, as if I had been given a second chance at happiness. I had been through many challenges and battles, and I had persevered and triumphed. Facing and overcoming what seemed like unsurmountable difficulties, both in life and on my trip, had forced me to draw on a deep reserve of inner strength and had opened up a world of possibilities that I was just now beginning to see. I had faced failure so many times and had been tempted to give up. But with God's grace and the support of many friends, I knew that I was blossoming into a stronger woman than I had ever thought possible, revealing an inner fortitude I had never believed I had. Rewarding as completing the Bun Burner ride itself was, this dawning awareness of who I was and what I could do was even more significant to me.

Enjoying the dazzling lights of DC, the Washington Monument, and a rooftop dinner with Ethan

CHAPTER FOUR

BLESSED BEYOND MEASURE

Days 15–19
Niagara Falls, New York, to Washington, DC

I am blessed to have three beautiful adult children whom I absolutely adore: twins Elliot and Eleanor and Ethan, who is six years older. All three children have my smile and their dad's blond hair, blue eyes, and tall stature. All are also distinctly and wonderfully unique. Ethan is gregarious, humorous, and a natural leader. He has always had the ability to gather a group of people together and convince them to embark on some grand adventure—and to be happy about doing it. Elliot is determined, resourceful, and entrepreneurial and has managed to develop a thriving business, even during this time of economic uncertainty. He is exceptionally goal driven and imaginative about accomplishing what he sets his mind to. Eleanor is generous, creative, and naturally gifted in the area of science. She has an innate ability to care for and work with animals and is always the first to notice when one is injured. I credit her with saving my life, as she was the one who first alerted me to my swollen lymph nodes, leading to my cancer diagnosis and subsequent treatment.

The children and I had all been together as a family at Christmas time during my cancer treatments, but after the holidays Ethan had returned to work in DC and the twins went back to their respective college campuses. Just a few weeks later, in early March, Elliot came home to live with me when his Oregon honors college went online due to COVID-19. Eleanor's school was in Southern California, near her father's house, and she went to his home when the pandemic hit and her campus also went online. She and I had both been hesitant for her to travel by plane to visit with me, but we were able to arrange transportation by car for her to visit me in June, before I left on my trip. She would also be coming to live with me for several months in the fall when I returned from my trip. However, I had been unable to see Ethan at all since December, and my heart was aching for me to be with him. It had not been feasible for me to drive to DC and back during the school year, and I was so grateful to be able to take my bike there during summer.

My longing for Ethan was so deep, it would be safe to say that there was nothing more important to me about my journey than making it to Washington, DC, to spend time with him. As I packed my gear to leave Niagara Falls on Wednesday, I realized it had only been two weeks since I had started my trip from home in Oregon. Part of what had propelled me to complete my "Bun Burner" ride from South Dakota to New York was the intense desire I had to see Ethan face to face and to do it sooner rather than later. I had planned my visit to coincide with the weekend so that he would be off work and we would able to spend time together. My trip south to him would take me through Pennsylvania, and a fellow rider had suggested that Lancaster might be a good place to stop for the night.

On the last leg of my 1,500-mile Bun Burner ride, I had noticed a rattling sound coming from my bike, so I stopped by the American Harley-Davidson dealership in North Tonawanda, New York, on my way to Lancaster. I explained to the mechanic that the rattling vanished when I pulled in the clutch and that I didn't notice the sound once I was in sixth gear. The service department did a test ride and said the rattling might be from the primary chain tensioner running a little high. However, they said the problem would most likely correct itself soon and I should be fine to drive to DC. They recommended I get the bike serviced while I was in DC, just to make sure everything was in order. The mechanic gave me a great compliment about my bike. He said, "Well, this isn't a touring bike, but you've made it out to be one!" I had picked my 2018 Softail Slim because of its lighter weight (compared to other Harleys), but I had it outfitted with saddlebags, a luggage rack, and two good-sized touring bags.

The bucolic farmland in Piffard, New York, provides a reassuring distraction from concerns about mechanical issues with the bike.

It is hard to think about the heat when gazing out at the cool,
lush, vast seas of green riding from Tioga, Pennsylvania.

It was hot and muggy as I traveled through New York
and then rural Pennsylvania, heading south to see my son,
but the vast vistas of endless green trees took my mind off
the heat. It was a little disconcerting that the bike continued
to make rattling noises in the lower gears. But I reassured
myself I had a plan in place to get it looked at more closely
in DC and focused on the beauty around me. I arrived in
Lancaster Wednesday evening, in time to eat at a locally
owned Trinidadian eatery called Callaloo. While on the
road, I typically eat out for lunch and dinner, and I am often
unfamiliar with local restaurants, so I rely on tips from locals,
bikers, and of course, Yelp. This establishment had a 4.5-star
Yelp rating and did not disappoint. I gorged on doubles street
food with fried bread and curried chick-peas, coconut jerk
chicken, and homemade ginger and lemongrass creme brûlée.
I realized that many tourists arriving in Lancaster would miss
out on this great food, opting instead for the more iconic
Amish eateries, but I was very happy with my decision.

TOURING TIP

On a long road trip, eating out for all meals can be more costly than many riders, myself included, can afford. I save money by eating lunch and dinner out and supplementing with snacks from local stores. I typically avoid purchasing food at gas stations because of the high markups there, and I seek out grocery stores instead. I have found non-dairy protein drinks to be a great mid-afternoon snack while on the road, as the drinks do not need to be refrigerated and the high levels of protein keep my energy up until I can eat dinner, so I buy several at a time and stow them in my bag. Once I've arrived in the town where I will be staying for the night, I buy snacks for after dinner and the next morning's breakfast. Not only do I save money, but I can sleep in and still be on the road at the same time as if I'd awakened early and gone out to breakfast.

I could have explored Amish country more the next day, but when I saw how close I already was to Washington, I decided to continue south and arrive in DC a night earlier than planned. I simply couldn't wait to see my son! I was delighted to find out that the nearest Harley-Davidson dealership was willing to take my bike for a few days and service it while I was with Ethan. Not only did the Harley-Davidson of Fort Washington, Maryland, offer me a discount on the service, but they saved me over $200 in DC parking fees. This is a great strategy to keep in mind while visiting any large city on a bike!

I was a little worried about arriving a day early and told my son I would completely understand if he was not able to see me until the following evening, but I was elated to hear that he wanted to see me that night. He suggested we meet on the corner of I Street and New Jersey Avenue, halfway between his apartment and my hotel in the Navy Yard area of Washington. I was bursting with anticipation and also, strangely, a little apprehensive. It had been so long since I had seen him, and I was nervous that I might not recognize him right away with his mask on, especially since there were so many people on the busy streets of DC. But the instant Ethan turned the corner, my heart leaped as I recognized his familiar gait and stride, not to mention his wavy blond hair. I tried not to appear too enthusiastic, as I knew it might embarrass him, but I jumped up and down with excitement and was very happy to be able to give him a big hug.

Grateful and relieved to see Ethan in Washington, DC, after months apart

After months apart, it was a relief and a joy to walk with him, talk with him, and hear about his life. Ethan suggested we go to the Capitol Building and then sit on the grass under a tree in the park right across from the Capitol. It was sunny and hot—still over nine-five degrees even in the evening— and I was very grateful to be able to rest in the shade and relax with him. The last time I had seen him, I was still married and going through cancer treatments with debilitating side effects. During that visit, we had eaten meals together as a family most nights, or rather, everybody else had. But I had been able only to watch everyone else eat, unable to swallow much of anything. My stress level at that time was high, and I knew I had not been myself around him or my other two children. This time with him felt like the beginning of a new start for us together.

After visiting in the park, we picked up some delicious burgers and fries to go and ate on the stunning roof-top patio of his apartment building. Sitting with my son over twelve floors up in the sky with a gorgeous view of a pink and purple sunset and the Capitol Building and Washington Monument lit up at night, I was literally and figuratively in heaven.

I was so very blessed to be able to spend the next three days in Washington, DC, with Ethan. We grilled steak on his roof-top patio, ate out, ordered food in, and explored the area near his building on foot. I purchased some things for his apartment and met one of his best friends. I tried riding an electric scooter on the sidewalk next to his apartment and discovered it's impossible for an inexperienced scooter rider to master the machine while holding a purse and a hoodie. The attempt was not all that successful. Next, I tried an electric bike, on which I was also a little shaky until my son said, "Mom, just pretend it's a motorcycle." I did, and it worked! We had time to relax together, talk together, and even play video games together. I have to say, though, I am much better at driving a motorcycle in real life than I am at steering one in a video game.

There is something about being with a loved one in person that is so much more fulfilling than talking by phone. I had missed Ethan so very deeply during the several months we had been apart, stranded on opposite coasts by the dangers of airplane travel in a global pandemic. I explain to all of my children that I love them equally, and at the same time individually. I have fond memories of my father telling me I was his favorite older daughter. It was a joke between us because he had two daughters and I was the only "oldest." Even with the phrase wrapped up in a joke, there was something comforting about hearing him say it—so much so that I have continued the tradition with my children. For instance, I tell my daughter she is my favorite daughter, and we both laugh because she is my only daughter. Similarly, with Ethan, I tell him he holds a special place in my heart because he was my first-born child and my only child for six and a half years. I homeschooled him when he was young, and I was able to take him camping, teach him how to ski, and spend extra time helping him learn, grow, and develop into the wonderful person that he is today.

Ethan was nine years old and the twins three when I became a single mother for the first time. Even though I have an MBA from a top-five business school, I chose to run a daycare in my home rather than return to corporate life, so that I could continue to be with my children during working hours. The twins were so young that I'm not even sure they knew I was "working." I think they were just happy to have other playmates around all the time. I have so many fond memories of taking my children along with the daycare children to the lake, the ocean, hiking, and exploring in general.

It wasn't realistic to continue the daycare business indefinitely because I needed to have healthcare benefits and a retirement plan. One day one of my clients said to me, "Kathleen, you're so good with children, why don't you become a teacher?" Her comment had an immediate impact on me, as it made all the sense in the world. I had learned through running the daycare that I loved caring for and nurturing other children. I also very much wanted a career that would allow me to take my children camping during the summer and on adventures during the weekends and other school holidays, something that would be possible if I taught in the same school district where my children attended.

I was able to find a reputable online teaching credential program that would allow me to do almost all of my schoolwork late at night while the children were sleeping. Within a few weeks, I had joined the program, and within ten months I had completed all of my course requirements. I started teaching my own high school math classes at Capistrano Valley High School that fall, when the twins entered kindergarten. I discovered I was passionate about teaching the same way I was passionate about parenting. In both situations, it was so very rewarding to make a positive difference in the lives of others.

Before I became a parent myself, I had no idea how much I would love my children. But from the moment Ethan was born I instantly felt a fierce, deep love for him that surpassed any emotion I had felt in the past. In fact, my love for him was so intense I was worried I would not be able to care for subsequent children as much. When the twins were born, however, I learned something new about love—unlike many things in life, it is not finite. In other words, I have an infinite amount of love to give to all my children.

In the midst of the pain from the cancer battle and my failing marriage, I had been struggling with feelings of hopelessness and despair. I wasn't sure if I would live or die, and the strain of trying to save a marriage torn by lies and betrayals was taking its toll. The gratitude journal I started shortly after the divorce was very therapeutic. It had helped me to focus on what I did have, rather than what I didn't have. By the time I arrived in Washington, DC, to visit Ethan, my outlook had already improved tremendously. But seeing him in person, hugging him, talking with him, and just being with him was a much-appreciated balm to my soul. It helped me to put into even sharper perspective how very much I had to be grateful for. I can think of nothing, other than my faith, that I am more appreciative for than my children.

I had briefly considered leaving DC early, because the weather forecast for my Monday departure was ninety-five degrees, along with rain, thunder, and lightning. I was nervous about putting on rain gear in extreme heat, as well as riding in such rough conditions. In the end, I decided I would rather take my chances dealing with heat and thunder than lose even one minute with my son. I was honored that he chose to see me off at my hotel Monday morning, even though it was a workday for him. I was able to get in one more hug before jumping into the Uber to the dealership.

TOURING TIP

I feel more comfortable riding my bike if I know I am prepared for all weather conditions as well as unexpected changes in plans. As a result, my personal policy is to have a wide variety of gear with me at all times, not only on long trips. One of my saddlebags is always filled with an emergency overnight bag (medication, toothbrush and toothpaste, sleep mask, makeup, and razor) as well as rain gear, extra layers, and a cooling vest. This bag is pre-packed, and I never remove the items unless I am using them or cleaning them.

On my ride over to the dealership, I reflected on how extraordinarily blessed I had been in the last few months. I had been able to beat throat cancer, navigate the choppy waters of a second divorce, find a way to teach my students during the pandemic, spend time with old friends, and make many new ones. I had managed to adjust my bike to fit my post-cancer body, outfit it with a luggage rack, and find new touring bags appropriate for my trip. At that point in the summer, I had already visited fourteen states, gone over 4,000 miles, completed two endurance rides, and eaten dozens of delicious meals. But the sweetest treat of all was spending time with my firstborn!

Surrounded by trees after feasting on mountain and
valley views on the Blue Ridge Parkway, Virginia

CHAPTER FIVE

I'VE GOT THIS!

Days 20–21
Washington, DC, to Tail of the Dragon

A common strategy for dealing with fears is facing them head on. However, riding a motorcycle involves literally putting your life in your own hands, which makes the stakes for dealing with riding-related fears even higher. Leaving on my solo cross-country trip, I was not only afraid of being alone—I was also worried my technical riding skills and general motorcycle knowledge were not up to the task. I had common concerns: Would I be able to navigate all the curves? Would I drop the bike or endanger myself in some way? Would I know what to do if there were technical issues with my bike?

I believe it is healthy to maintain a certain level of concern about operating a motorcycle. It helps me to stay alert, be intentional about my actions, and exercise the appropriate level of caution. For instance, when I asked the service writer at the dealership in North Tonawanda, if my bike was safe to ride south, he laughed and said, "No, it's not. It's never 'safe' to ride a bike." I re-phrased my question to ask whether my bike was mechanically sound to ride to DC and got an affirmative response that time. Point well taken.

In any case, I had taken steps to develop my riding ability and motorcycle knowledge in general. As mentioned, when first obtaining my motorcycle endorsement, I had taken three private lessons in addition to the weekend-long, state-approved Team Oregon driver's training. By the time I left on this trip, I had logged over 26,000 bike-driving miles in the two years since obtaining my license. The previous summer I had tackled several notable roads on my own bike, including the Million Dollar Highway, Beartooth Highway, and Needles Highway. My over 60,000 miles on the back of a bike over the previous four years-plus had given me general knowledge about how to deal with a variety of problems that can come up on the road. Since my divorce in February, I had also gone on many solo day trips without a single incident of concern.

But I still felt an overall lack of confidence in my general riding ability and motorcycle knowledge. Looking back, I think a lot of the reason I was scared was that many times my ex-husband had yelled and sworn at me while I was driving my bike. On many occasions, as I was backing up my bike in a parking lot, pulling over, or following the directions on the app on my phone, he would scream at me, call me names, and make embarrassing comments, sometimes while others could see and hear. It was impossible to predict when these outbursts would occur, and they happened both on and off the bike. On more than one occasion, strangers had asked me if I needed help or if they should call the police.

I knew it wasn't right for me to be treated this way. I did seek help from a women's support group and learned to remove myself from the situation, practice self-care, and try not to internalize the attacks when they came. But I was frightened to tell most people about what was really going on. I was embarrassed about how I was allowing myself to be treated and yet afraid to leave him and live alone. I also kept thinking that things would improve. So, I tried to compartmentalize the problems but was often unsuccessful. One time while shopping with my daughter at Target, she said, "Mom, I know you're trying to act happy and have a good time with me. But I can tell that you're hurting, and I can see the Kleenex pieces on your face from when you must have been crying earlier."

So not only did I doubt my riding abilities, but I also doubted my strength as a person. However, a miraculous thing happened when I started my cancer treatments in December of 2019. The radiation burned the inside and outside of my throat, and I was so sore that I could not eat. Soon after, I really couldn't even drink water—I could only sip enough to take medication. I had to sleep sitting up so I wouldn't choke. I was on three different pain killers and still hurt so badly that sometimes I would cry. My voice grew hoarse, and then I lost it completely for a time. Yet the physical pain was a walk in the park compared to the emotional pain and trauma I had been dealing with for years in my marriage. As people encouraged me throughout my cancer battle, though, I started to feel more self-assured in general.

My children, friends, colleagues, students, and their parents told me they were proud of me for battling the throat cancer. They said I was a strong person for enduring the radiation and chemotherapy treatments and that they were grateful I was still teaching. The IT and performance arts departments at school outfitted me with equipment to amplify my voice while I could still speak. I missed only six days of work during the two months of treatment, mainly because I so much enjoyed being with my students and also because it was easier to distract myself from pain when I was teaching. After coming back from my longest absence, of four days, my advanced algebra students actually clapped when they saw me walk into the classroom. The support and encouragement from friends, students, and colleagues during this time was a crucial factor in giving me enough emotional strength to file for divorce.

After the divorce, I gradually started feeling more hopeful in general. My confidence in my riding abilities also improved as I started getting affirming, positive words from other riders. After my husband moved out in February, I joined two local Harley Owners Groups (HOG chapters) and started looking there for riding partners.

I met Leo Guzman Fernandez, a fellow HOG member, at a Harley dealership, and he started inviting me on rides. Leo is a genial, friendly, positive person who seems to make every event a party. He is one of the most talented riding leaders I have ever met. His twinkling eyes and wide smile belie what could be his rather intimidating tattoos, full black beard, and red skeleton face mask, often worn to protect his face from the elements during rides. After reading about my cancer battle, he included me in his private Facebook riding group chat and said, "You are a warrior. I have seen cancer very close and admire you for what you have done and continue to do. It is an honor to ride with you." His comments gave me a much-needed boost of self-esteem at a time when I was worried I would not be able to find riding partners.

Another HOG member and riding friend, Rod Myer, was also encouraging. When meeting with me to tell me about his Black Sheep group, he declared, "Kathleen, you may not realize this, but you are a good rider." Rod's comment was affirming to me both because it was completely unsolicited and because he is the kind of person who measures his words and means what he says. Rod has an intensity of expression and a seriousness that make his comments seem genuine. He is also an experienced biker and active within the biking community as the Oregon regional director for Black Sheep Harley-Davidsons for Christ.

My interactions with the director of the Rose City HOG, Grant Myers, had also been instrumental in building my confidence. Grant was one of the first people to accept an invitation from me to go for a ride when I posted the request on our group's Facebook page. At the time, I had no idea what kind of person he was, other than that he was a leader of my HOG chapter. I remember some of my girlfriends were a little horrified that I would ride alone to the beach with a complete stranger. But my intuition told me it would be safe to go with him. I also reasoned if there were any problems, I could just drive away!

Grant and I ended up having a great time driving to Seaside and back. We are different in many ways—Grant is much taller, is retired, has a background in the Air Force, and tends to speak with his actions rather than his words. But from the very beginning Grant made it a point to create riding opportunities for me and to make them enjoyable. He is extremely easy going and, like Leo, willing to drive longer distances, which is important to me. Grant often asks me what kind of a ride I would like to go on and then takes the time to plan one. His kindness, generosity and supportiveness towards my riding have helped me to believe more in my own riding abilities. After one fun, curve-filled ride to The Dalles, Leo, Grant, and I stopped to eat lunch together, and Leo commented, "I am so proud of you for how well you are riding."

Fueled by those words of encouragement, as well as my passion for driving and my desire to see my son in Washington, DC, I had headed east on my own. As the days progressed, my confidence grew. The first real riding challenge of this summer had been my trip over Beartooth Highway, leaving Yellowstone on my way to Red Lodge. It was more of a challenge for me this year than it had been the year before, because there were such strong crosswinds. However, the road was in excellent condition, and I found it fairly manageable, despite the tight turns and steep grade.

My next real challenge was the Needles Highway in Custer State Park, South Dakota. One particular turn there had troubled me the previous summer—a tight turn on a grade with a five mile per hour posted advised speed. I had messaged Leo the night before making the turn this year, asking for his advice. His response was, "Please don't even think about it. You can do it. You are a very good rider. Just don't be afraid of taking it easy." He reminded me of some cornering tips, but it was his encouragement that helped me the most. When I took the turn the next day, it was so much easier than I had remembered.

Taking the long, curvy route to The Dalles for lunch—Grant, Leo, and me smiling for the camera at the Rowena Crest viewpoint on the Historic Columbia River Highway, west of Rowena

The next milestone in building my riding confidence on this trip occurred when I picked up my bike at the Harley dealership outside of Washington, DC. I had been a little embarrassed about having it serviced just because of a rattling noise I had heard, and if it really was just the primary chain tensioner being a little on the high side, a service really wasn't necessary yet. But my intuition told me it was better to err on the side of safety, and when I picked up the bike, the service writer said that the clutch had been way out of adjustment, two full rotations past what it should have been! It actually boosted my morale to know that I had discerned there really had been something wrong with the bike. In addition, my comment to him about the noise going away when I pulled in the clutch had been helpful in diagnosing the problem.

The biggest technical challenge of my summer ride was now looming on the horizon—the Tail of the Dragon on the border between North Carolina and Tennessee. I was both excited and nervous about the prospect of navigating this road on my own bike, as it is arguably one of the most difficult riding challenges in the country. Filled with over 300 curves in eleven miles and no intersecting roads, the Tail attracts hundreds of drivers a day in peak months. I had ridden this curvy stretch of road in 2015 on the back of a bike and seen firsthand the "tree of shame," where motorcyclists can leave the parts from their wrecked bikes—victims of this high-crash area. So, as I left DC and headed south to North Carolina, I found myself contemplating how I would perform when I arrived at the Tail the following night.

Farmlands in Stanley, Virginia, on the way to the famous
Blue Ridge Parkway, are picturesque in their own right.

After leaving the Harley dealership, I headed toward Front Royal, Virginia, to eat at Spelunker's, a local hamburger joint located near the north entrance of the Shenandoah National Park. They serve hamburgers with five-ounce patties blended from chuck and brisket, ground in house daily. The patties, juicy and dripping with just the right amount of fat, are definitely worth the stop. I planned to ride the Blue Ridge Parkway about eighty miles south of Front Royal and debated whether to take Skyline Drive from Front Royal to get there. I decided to save the twenty-five dollar entrance fee required for motorcyclists and take Highway 340 south to the head of the parkway in Waynesboro, Virginia, instead. I knew I would see similar vistas of the Appalachian Mountains from there and preferred to save a little money toward lodging that night.

The Blue Ridge Parkway was one of my "must-do" items because of the spectacular mountain views and absence of large trucks. Although I love the views, I hadn't planned on doing the entire stretch down to Cherokee, North Carolina, simply because the forty-five mile per hour speed limit and preponderance of curves would have meant getting to the Tail of the Dragon much later the next day than I preferred. So I booked a hotel room at Fancy Gap, about halfway down the parkway, and then took Interstate 81 part of the way. That decision turned out to be fortuitous, because most of the parkway was under construction, with hard-packed gravel rather than smooth road. Even though driving such a long stretch on gravel was tiring, it also bolstered my confidence that I had made it so far with no incidents.

There was severe rain from Fancy Gap to Robbinsville, and other motorcyclists were pulled over under an overpass. However, I had my rain gear on and decided to continue in the hope of making it to Deals Gap Motorcycle Resort at the start of the Tail in time to "slay the dragon" that night. I was elated to find that by the time I reached Robbinsville, the rain had stopped. I dropped off my bags at the hotel and drove straight to the Tail around 5:45 PM.

TOURING TIP
To ride Tail of the Dragon, I prefer to leave from Robbinsville, North Carolina. Many motorcyclists I talked to recommended staying in Cherokee, North Carolina, at the end of the Blue Ridge Parkway. That town has an abundance of attractions, including fine dining and gambling, but it is over an hour away from the start of the Tail. Robbinsville is less than half an hour away and also located almost directly at the beginning of the Cherohala Skyway.

The timing ended up being ideal. One of the challenges of the course is that it attracts many varieties of motorcyclists and sports car enthusiasts, and the higher traffic levels and the varying speeds of the other motorists involved can complicate an already difficult course. I had planned to wait at the resort until there was a lull in traffic, as I had done in 2015, when I was riding on the back of a bike. But apparently the rain had kept many people away. When I arrived to find the resort almost empty, I headed straight up Highway 129 without stopping, following the Tail into Tennessee.

"Slaying the Dragon" on Tail of the Dragon in Tennessee, an iconic route for motorcycle and sports car enthusiasts

The ride was exhilarating! The challenge came at me from both the shape and condition of the road. It seemed to curve in three directions: left to right, up and down, and diagonally. I would be heading into a curve, going down a hill, and coming in at an angle, and then out of nowhere I'd see a pothole in the middle of the turn. The fact that I hadn't stopped at the resort before the ride meant that I didn't have time to strategize or worry, so instead of thinking about problems that might come up, I focused on using good technique and enjoying the ride. I pulled over at the end to take pictures next to a road sign that said, "Motorcycles—high crash area next 11 miles."

After taking my pictures, I turned the bike around and headed back onto the Tail for a rare treat—I was able to do almost the entire course with no traffic! It was glorious to have the road to myself and to be able to go exactly the speed I wanted without anyone behind or in front of me. I got a souvenir shirt at the resort and then celebrated with a refreshing iceberg wedge salad at the Tapoco Lodge Tavern, just six minutes away.

Celebrating victory after successfully navigating
over 300 curves in eleven miles

Back at the tavern, I sat next to the Cheoah River and savored my accomplishment, reflecting on how much my life had changed since I had last been to the Tail of the Dragon five years earlier. Back then I had been a rider on the back of a bike, never thinking that I'd be brave enough, strong enough, or skilled enough to ride my own motorcycle. In my wildest dreams, I never would have imagined I would not only eventually own my own bike, but also be able to successfully ride one of the most challenging roads in the country.

In some ways, I felt as if completing the Tail of the Dragon was a rite of passage, a defining moment where I could comfortably identify as being a "biker," in my own right. In the back of my mind in the weeks leading up to the Tail, I was harboring doubts about my ability to complete the course safely. Successfully riding the Tail on my own, not just once but twice, turned my focus from what I might not be able to do to what I had actually done. But this shift in perspective wasn't just about my bike-riding abilities. As I proved to myself that I could direct and guide my 700-pound bike safely through a variety of technically challenging courses, I was also becoming more self-assured in my ability to handle difficulties in general.

Leaving on my trip just a few weeks earlier, I had been uncertain how I would handle traveling on my own. Not only had I successfully dealt with mechanical problems, poor road conditions, and challenging courses but, even more significantly, I was thriving on the solitude from my solo travel. After years of staying in an unhealthy marriage due to a crippling fear of being alone, I was finding unspeakable freedom in the knowledge that I had all the companionship I needed within me. It had taken courage to leave on the trip, not knowing how I would fare emotionally with the lack of human company, but I could already see that I was much more independent than I ever thought possible. I was transforming before my own eyes into a more capable, competent woman than ever before. I had faced the fiery battle of cancer head-on, risen like a phoenix from the ashes of the death of my marriage, and was soaring with the wind beneath my wings.

Ready to hit the road again—parked in Ouray, Colorado,
for lunch after riding Million Dollar Highway

CHAPTER SIX

DON'T LET OBSTACLES STAND IN THE WAY OF DREAMS

Days 22–25
Tail of the Dragon to Silverton, Colorado

Mishaps or unexpected obstacles are bound to happen on any road trip. Sitting in my hotel room plotting my course after completing Trail of the Dragon, I struggled to find a place I could go next that didn't have poor weather. I looked at the weather in over a dozen cities and got the same forecast: rain and lightning for the next ten days, so I decided to call my friend, Grant Myers. He's great at pulling information from his computer and always willing to lend a hand, but the report he sent was not encouraging. Basically, the entire Southeast was predicted to have bad weather for more than a week.

I had a few options: stay put and read good books for several days, stay in the Southeast and drive in inclement weather, or head toward the other side of the country and use weather conditions as motivation to complete another Iron Butt Association (IBA) ride.

I decided to go for it. After all, for me this trip was about celebrating life, overcoming obstacles, and proving to myself that I had a hope and a future to look forward to, something I knew that God had promised (see note), even though I hadn't been able to see it earlier. I had so enjoyed my first Bun Burner 1500 ride, and I had my eye on a nice stretch of interstate running west from a town near Knoxville, Tennessee. I had originally hoped to stay in the Southeast, ride the Natchez Trace Parkway, and visit New Orleans. However, it didn't look like there would be much visibility on the parkway for days to come. Although going west now also meant I would miss my favorite breakfast place in New Orleans, Ruby Slippers, it didn't justify staying in the poor weather. I was determined to enjoy myself and make something of the trip, regardless of whatever weather came my way.

NOTE

"For I know the plans I have for you," declares the Lord, "plans to prosper you and not to harm you, plans to give you hope and a future." (NIV)

                            —Jeremiah 29:11, The Holy Bible

I had learned a few major lessons from my first IBA ride. One of them was that I would be safer traveling west than east, because I would have more daylight hours. The second was the value of calling ahead to make sure that gas stations would be open when I arrived. During my downtime in Washington, DC, I had plotted out potential gas stops and called to confirm their hours. I had picked the potential course from Monterey, Tennessee, going west on Interstate 40 about 1,300 miles to Albuquerque, New Mexico, and then turning north for another 260 miles on Highway 550 to Colorado. The route ended in one of my favorite towns, Silverton, Colorado. Silverton had been on my "must-do" list for each of the previous five summers, as it is the starting point for one of the most epic rides in the country—the Million Dollar Highway.

With a general plan in mind, I plotted my course from the Tail to the starting point of my next IBA endurance ride, Monterey, Tennessee.

The next day ended up being spectacular. Early the next morning, before the rain was predicted to hit, I headed north on Highway 129 from Robbinsville for a little less than ten miles and then west on the Cherohala Skyway. This national scenic byway is forty-three miles long and passes through the Cherokee National Forest and the Nantahala National Forest on its way to Tellico Plains, Tennessee. The road runs along the top of a ridge with breathtaking mountain and forest views on both sides.

The drive along the Skyway was refreshing and inspiring— almost no traffic, and the vegetation was lush and vibrant. I stopped at an overlook to admire the view and noticed several Red-Spotted Purple Admiral butterflies mating. They were flitting, flying, and dancing and shimmering in the sunlight. The air was moist and crisp, as there had been significant rain the day before. I breathed in the fresh, earth-rich air and took in all of the beautiful sights around me.

Getting back on the bike, I noticed that the road was in such great condition I could swoop, swirl, and zoom around curves and corners without dropping to fourth gear. It was like skiing on butter. I felt like a rebel, out riding my bike even though severe thunder and lightning was forecast for days. What a find! I resolved to spend a lot more time riding in Tennessee during future summer trips.

At the end of the Skyway, I stopped at a Harley store to get a tank top and met another group of nine bikers, also picking up souvenirs. When I exited the store, I found one of the bikers, Teresa Smith, waiting for me with the rest of the group all lined up behind her on the porch. I was a little surprised to see them, as they had finished their shopping several minutes before I had. Teresa asked if I was traveling alone, and when I told her I was, she turned to the rest of her friends and nodded her head. I got the sense that they had all been waiting for me to come out so they could ask about my situation. She introduced herself and asked if she could be my Facebook friend, and I gladly gave her my information. It was not unusual for people to want to know more about my solo travels, and I found that sharing my story with others boosted my confidence a great deal.

Another great view after an already spectacular day—the farmlands of Sweetwater, Tennessee, on the way from the Cherohala Parkway and the Tellico Grains Bakery to the start of the endurance ride in Monterey, Tennessee

Back home, when the trip was over, I decided to follow up with Teresa and ask her about that day—about the nod and what it meant. She confirmed that I had read the circumstances correctly, that I had been the source of discussion within her group. Apparently, she told her other friends, "I really think that lady over there is riding by herself. I'm going to find out." I asked her what had prompted her to speak with me. She said, "I thought it was so cool that you had the courage to travel alone. A lot of times we think we will do something like that, and then we don't." She said her impression of me at the time was, "She wasn't going to let anything stop her from doing what she needed to do, to be what she needed to be." I got goose bumps when I heard this, because my first interaction with her had occurred in the section of my trip where I was learning about the value of overcoming obstacles—she was right on!

I absolutely adore baked goods and was so excited to find a five-star rated bakery just a few minutes away from the Harley store. The minute I walked into the Tellico Grains Bakery I knew I had found another "must-do" stop while riding in Tennessee. The food is all made fresh daily on the premises in small batches, and it looked and smelled delicious. I bought a wood-fired bacon and pepperoni pizza for lunch, a New York-style cheesecake for dessert, and a cookie and granola for snacking on the go. The owner was also named Kathleen and kept joking that I could stay as long as I wanted, but after I finished eating, with rain imminent, I put on rain gear and headed west through farmlands to my hotel in Monterey, Tennessee. I used the evening to organize my gear and rest up to start my second nested endurance ride the next day.

I left Monterey around 9:30 on Thursday morning after gassing up, documenting my mileage, and getting my witness statements signed. I had decided the night before that it would not be efficient or safe to pull over regularly on the interstate to put on and take off rain gear. Since it was going to be in the 90s, I resolved that I would ride through the rain without the gear and trust that the wind and heat would keep me relatively dry. I knew that I could always change my plans if necessary. I was rained on during almost every segment of the first 1,000 miles but was not at any time uncomfortable. In fact, the rain felt very refreshing, and I found a sense of freedom in being wet and relishing it.

Everything went without a hitch for the first 200 miles, but when I stopped at the Love's Travel Center in Jackson,

Tennessee, the pump was not accepting credit cards outside, and I had to wait in line to pay. Then I had to wait again to get my receipt. After walking outside with my receipt, I noticed that it did not have a time stamp on it anywhere, required documentation for the IBA. So I waited in line a third time to ask the cashier to note the time and sign the receipt. At that point, I called a manager at Love's and asked why there were no time stamps on the in-store receipts, and she said it was because they have so many professional truckers who use their stores. This created a wrinkle in my plans, as I was on a timed trip and really did not want to risk having to wait in line three times every time I gassed up at a Love's. So I called up my good friend, Kathy Nesper, and asked if she could scout out alternative gas stations to replace the Love's centers I had previously included on my itinerary.

Touring Tip

One of the things that makes road trips fun for me is having a great support network. I am blessed to have a lot of friends who ride, as well as friends who don't ride but are supportive. I know that I can call on them when an unexpected need comes up and am honored to return the favor when they need assistance. Whenever a friend asks for a favor, I try to make their request a priority. For instance, my friend, Leo, left on a road trip a few weeks after mine and called asking for information about various stops and accommodations along the way. I made the effort to get him the information he needed in a timely manner, both because he is a friend and because I know he would do the same for me.

I continued west on Interstate 40, typically stopping every 130 to 160 miles to gas up, document my stop, and drink a protein drink. As on my earlier IBA ride, I encountered strong crosswinds and road construction at various times. But it was a wonderful change of pace to ride just for the sake of riding, without any special sightseeing or food stops to plan my ride around. I pulled into my second-to-last stop for the night at the Flying J in Sayre, Oklahoma, around 1:30 in the morning. As I drove up to the pump, I couldn't help but notice swarms of locusts everywhere. My bike was making crunching sounds as it ran over the ones on the pavement, and there were locusts buzzing all around me. When I lifted up the gas nozzle handle, one was sitting right next to my hand. I screamed and it jumped off, but the one on the end of the nozzle wouldn't leave. The most surreal thing about this experience was when I asked two gentlemen nearby what type of bugs they were. Their response: "What bugs?" It was as if I was in an Alfred Hitchcock movie and no one but I noticed.

Perhaps the most memorable stop to document miles on the endurance ride—the Flying J in Sayre, Oklahoma, at 1:30 in the morning was swarming with locusts.

The view was just too beautiful to resist—taking a quick break to capture the multi-colored mountainous panorama in San Ysidro, New Mexico, over 1,300 miles from the start of the endurance ride in Monterey, Tennessee, just the morning before.

After gassing up and documenting the end of my 1,000 miles at the Toot'n Totum in Amarillo, I checked into my room at 4:18 AM for a few hours of sleep. The next morning, tired but exhilarated, I left Amarillo around nine o'clock and continued west on Interstate 40 for almost 300 miles before turning north on Interstate 25 and then north again on US 550 North. When I reached Durango, Colorado, I stopped to document my miles and get my witness statement, as I had already driven more than the required 1,500 miles in less than thirty-six hours and wasn't sure if I would make it all the way to Silverton in time to document everything there. I was excited, tired, and relieved when I did, indeed, pull into Silverton around 6:30 PM, almost two hours earlier than necessary to qualify for my second Bun Burner certification.

There is a palpable sense of elation at the end of an Iron Butt ride, knowing that you have overcome obstacles, persevered through trials, and accomplished something significant. For me, though, the first order of business is taking care of paperwork. The IBA requires documentation at every step of the way, as well as two signed witness statements, one at the beginning and one at the end of your trip. One of the two employees at the gas station was on break when I arrived, and it took a few minutes for me to get both of the signatures I needed. Afterward, however, I allowed myself to luxuriate in the victory. I took a few pictures of me at the pump, turned around to admire the mountain views, and gazed longingly at the beginning of the Million Dollar Highway, just a few yards from where I stood. The parking lot of the station was covered in loose gravel and mud, and the bike and I were both dirty and grimy, but I was grinning from ear to ear.

In high spirits in Silverton, Colorado, after completing another Iron Butt Association-certified ride

I was so proud of myself for persevering through rain, crosswinds, gas stop receipt issues, road construction, the swarming locusts, and the challenge of covering so many miles in so little time. When both of my Bun Burner 1500 rides were certified, I would be eligible for "Mile Eater" status with the IBA. I thought that the most difficult part of the week was over. Little did I know that the next twenty-four hours would be even harder than the endurance ride!

By the time I checked into the Avon Hotel in Silverton on July 24, it was after 8 PM, and I knew many restaurants in the small town would soon be closing. After gassing up, I had gotten a few pictures on the main street of Silverton and grabbed some snacks at the grocery store. At check in, I paid for the night, and the hotel clerk offered to help me carry my motorcycle bags up to my room on the third floor. After setting my bags on the bed, he turned to me and said, "You know this is a shared room, right?" I was speechless. After all, I had just traveled halfway across the country and was looking forward to a delicious meal and a good night's sleep, not sharing a room with a stranger.

I didn't expect to share my hotel room with a stranger after traveling through six states in less than a day and a half.

The problem was that all the hotels in town were fully booked, it was getting dark, and there were no towns nearby that would be safe for me to ride to, especially being so tired. When I had made my reservation the day before, I had found the only room left in the entire town, even after checking all three of my booking apps. There was literally nothing I could do but try to make the best of the situation.

TOURING TIP
I keep several booking apps on my phone so that I can quickly and easily make reservations while on the road. Each app has its benefits, though I find the Booking.com app to be the most user friendly and consistently reliable way to find the best priced room. After booking a few stays on the platform, they begin offering "genius" discounts on future bookings. I also used the Hotel.com app a few times but do not find it as user friendly, although they do offer a free booking for every ten bookings completed through them. I downloaded the Hotel Tonight app and checked it several times, but it never yielded a better deal than the others in the cities I wanted to stay in.

A young man came in a few minutes later, mortified that he had left his things all over the room, because he didn't know it was a shared room either! We each had read the description, and it had not been clear to either of us that we would be sharing a bunkbed. The lack of privacy, risk of theft, and potential disruption to sleep were all issues for me, but my bigger concern was being in such close quarters with a stranger during a pandemic. I had just survived throat cancer, and my immune system was potentially weakened by the chemo and radiation. I tried to convince myself that this was just another part of my adventure, and in my nightly check-in with Kathy I told her this was nothing compared to getting throat cancer and going through a divorce.

Needless to say, neither the young man nor I got much sleep that night. The next morning, I called the manager to see if he had another room available. Not only did he say no, but he told me two new men would be joining me that night and then two different people the following day! I was exhausted from traveling and from getting so little sleep for two nights in a row and did not know what to do. I was determined to stay in Silverton for at least two more nights, because there was so much I wanted to do in the area, but I knew it would not be safe to stay in the room again due to my weakened immune system.

Fortunately, that morning while I was in line at the post office waiting to mail my ride documentation to the IBA, I shared my plight with the lady next to me, who happened to own some cabins north of town. Although it turned out that she didn't have a room available for more than one night, her manager knew of someone who might. When I called Red Mountain Motel & RV Park and explained my dire circumstances, the clerk offered me my own private cabin for the next three nights. I still had to pack up all my things, get The Avon hotel to agree to refund me for the two nights I wouldn't use, confirm the refund with Hotel.com, lug all my things from the third floor downstairs to my bike, pack them up, drive over to the new cabin, check in there, find a way to park my bike in the loose gravel, and unpack my things again.

The experience was emotionally and physically draining, especially working on so little sleep from the night before. By the time I finally got settled, I was tempted to just rest in my room for the remainder of the afternoon. But I looked out my window, saw the road to the Million Dollar Highway beckoning in the distance, and knew I could not miss the opportunity to ride it that day.

Riding the Million Dollar Highway is the pinnacle of joy for me. The first time I rode it, on the back of my now ex-husband's bike in 2015, I held my breath most of the way. The hairpin turns, figure eights, sheer drop-offs with no guard rails, and epic mountain and valley views make this part of the San Juan Skyway a stand out. I have ridden it every summer since then, the year before this trip for the first time on my own Harley. So, even though I was exhausted from my hotel woes, all of my troubles were left behind when I put my bike in gear and headed up this epic stretch of road between Silverton and Ouray.

The magnificent mountain views, sheer drop-offs and hairpin turns make the Million Dollar Highway a "must-do" item every summer.

Arriving in Ouray, I grabbed lunch at a pub in town then stopped at Mouse's Chocolates & Coffees for one of their "scrap" cookies. These delicious sugar cookies include scraps of homemade Belgian truffles, toffee, nuts, and dried fruit. Feeling properly fortified, I rode the Million Dollar Highway back to Silverton so I could experience the road the other direction and also make plans for the night. I planned to finish the evening with a loop from Silverton to Ouray and then around to Telluride and back to Silverton via Durango. However, after leaving Ouray that evening, I decided to spend some time relaxing at a hot springs instead and turn around in time to get a good dinner back in Silverton. By the end of the day, I had actually ridden the Million Dollar Highway four times. What a treat!

That night, after a great dinner at the Eureka Station, I reflected on how lucky I was. It had been a challenging year for many reasons—throat cancer, a second divorce, teaching through the pandemic, preparing myself and my bike for a big solo trip, and managing all of the unexpected difficulties that had come up. However, through faith, perseverance, and determination, I had so far managed to complete two Bun Burner 1500 rides, visit my son, travel through twenty-two states, and have the time of my life on some of the most exhilarating roads in the country. I knew that I would always face obstacles, both in life and on my trips, but I was also developing the confidence, strength, and skills to not let these hurdles keep me from my dreams.

Feeling indescribable newfound joy at
Rocky Mountain National Park, Colorado

CHAPTER SEVEN

EXPERIENCING NEW HEIGHTS OF JOY

Days 26–31
Silverton, Colorado, to Red Stone, Colorado

Not too many people know this, but I love to sing while I am riding. There is something about the joy, peace, and thrill of riding my bike, as well as a generous appreciation for the beauty of God's creation, that motivates me. I often sing to myself silently, but other times I belt out tunes over the roar of my motorcycle. My favorites are songs like "America the Beautiful," "The Star-Spangled Banner," and "Amazing Grace." The good news is that even though I'm tone-deaf, no one but God can hear.

I decided to research the history behind "America the Beautiful" when I started writing this chapter about my summer trip, as I remembered singing that song so many times during the joyous week I spent exploring Colorado. I was amazed, but perhaps not surprised, to find that the song was penned over a century earlier by another female teacher also inspired by her summer cross-country travel to Colorado!

Colorado encourages and rejuvenates me. I love Oregon and have no desire to move. However, I have always thought, at least since I started biking in Colorado, that it would be my second choice as a place to live. The riding is spectacular, the air crisp and cool, the mountains both comforting and majestic, and the colors amazing. I love the juxtaposition of the red earth, blue sky, green trees, white-capped mountains, and blue-green streams.

I was a little concerned about how I might feel about my time in Colorado this year, as I had so many memories of time spent there with my ex-husband on our cross-country trips the previous five summers. We had many favorite roads, restaurants, photo spots, and one particular inn that we especially liked. I was conflicted about whether to revisit the places I knew and loved or to avoid them entirely, because I didn't know if being in familiar places would bring back memories of lies and betrayals, pain and hardship, or if I would find those same places healing.

In the spirit of the trip itself—celebrating life and overcoming adversity—I decided to embrace the state wholeheartedly, visiting all the places I had loved before and discovering a few new ones. I was not disappointed in the decision. In fact, I was surprised, elated, and relieved to find that I discovered new heights of joy while crisscrossing this colorful state on my own.

My vacation in Colorado started in earnest on the morning of my second full day there, after getting a good night's sleep in a cabin where I did not need to share my bed (and air) with a stranger. I woke up on a beautiful Sunday morning, greeted by sunshine peeking through the red-checkered curtains on my cabin windows, a welcome relief after days of rain during my travels from Tennessee. I was so happy to see the sun that I left without putting on any makeup, not that I generally wear that much.

I savored every moment of this fifth ride on the Million Dollar Highway to Ouray for lunch. There were fewer clouds than the day before, and I had more unobstructed views of the mountains as I rode. That twenty-five-mile stretch of highway between Silverton and Ouray is one of the highest paved roads in Colorado and provides views of three different mountain ranges—the Coal Bank, Molas, and Red Mountain Passes. The road also travels through the Uncompahgre Gorge, with switchbacks through deep vertical canyons, towering jagged peaks overhead, and a beautiful river forging below. There is so much to feast on visually that it is easy to inadvertently lose track of the road. As I was heading north that morning, transfixed by the sight of an enormous waterfall running down the mountain to my left, I had to abruptly adjust my speed in the curve.

After arriving in Ouray, I lucked out and got a small table outdoors on the patio of the Colorado Boy Southwest Pub, with a great view of Main Street and the mountains beyond. I ordered a Detroit-style pepperoni pizza and savored the crispy crust and rich sauce while watching the hustle and bustle of the sidewalk traffic in the quaint little town. It was almost seventy degrees, and with the sun out in full force after days of rain, it was so relaxing and delightful to take my time eating, look at my map of Colorado, and think about what adventures I wanted to embark on over the next couple days.

The afternoon ride was rejuvenating and relaxing as I continued north on Highway 550 to Ridgway, west on Highway 62, and south on Highway 145 to Telluride. I traveled through picturesque farmlands, pastures, and bright green meadows. In the distance I could see tree-covered hills, mountain valleys, snow-capped peaks, and a bright blue sky.

I completed the loop by going south to Dolores and Durango and then north again to Silverton, transfixed by the views of red-colored cliffs and hills, blue streams, and a guest appearance from a local beaver. I had stopped at an AT&T store in Durango to get a replacement screen protector for my phone and encountered rain, hail, thunder, and lightning on my way back to Silverton. But I was snug as a bug with my heated electric jacket and rain gear, and so happy to be on my bike in such a beautiful part of the country.

Rediscovering the picturesque farmlands and
mountains on the loop through Telluride

TOURING TIP

If I'm going to be gone more than a few days, I like to pack backups for essential items that do not take up much space. It's very common for things to break or be stolen, and it's nice to have replacements handy instead of taking time out of my trip to go find them. For example, since I use a Ram XGrip to mount my phone on my bike, I always take an extra tether and rubber tips, as the tether will sometimes break and the tips can come off. I also take an extra face shield for my helmet, because it takes virtually no space in my bag when I stand it upright and pack my compression bags around it. I pack extra straps for my luggage in case a strap breaks or I change how I want to tie the bags down. A warranty on my

phone screen protector allows me to replace it at any AT&T
store, instead of having it mailed to my house. In addition, I
have back-up goggles, my winter pair of gloves as extras, and
additional layers in case my electric jacket fails. On this trip,
I ended up needing everything except my back-up goggles
and two layers.

To be honest, I had forgotten about the Telluride loop,
although I realized that day that I had done it at least once
before. My ex-husband is much more of a born navigator than
I am. Even though I was familiar with much of the country
from my previous five summer trips with him, part of the
journey for me on this trip was learning to do my own research.
It was such a pleasure to rediscover this loop on my own.

One of my favorite ways to plan rides for the days ahead is
to confer with other bikers or locals who are familiar with the
area. When I had first arrived in Silverton two nights before, I
had been lucky enough to encounter local Sharon Vann while
I was eating dinner at the Eureka Station. She saw me in my
biking gear with my map on the dinner table and came over
and introduced herself. We hit if off right away, and she soon
started writing all kinds of fun tips on my map with my pen.
The loop to Telluride and back was her idea, as was the ride
the following day.

Touring Tip

A paper map is an invaluable conversation starter, in a way
a phone could never be. I have found that having an open
map out on the table while I am eating is a great way to
make myself approachable to others and start conversations
I might not otherwise have had. People notice my riding gear
and the map and often ask where I am from or where I am
going. I highlight my route with a different color highlighter
than the points of interest I marked earlier, so I have a handy
visual reference of where I have been. Of course, on this trip
many people also wanted to know if I was traveling alone. I

*very much enjoy the back-and-forth conversations, as well
as information sharing and encouragement exchanged with
others on my travels*

Monday, I headed north along the Million Dollar Highway
again, this time to the Black Canyon of the Gunnison National
Park, just seventy-five miles away. What a treat! This national
park features a paved road that follows twelve miles of the
forty-eight-mile-long canyon through some of the steepest,
deepest, and oldest gorges in America. The canyon, sculpted
by the Gunnison River, can be viewed from both the north
and south rims at twelve different overlooks that feature
beautifully striated, colorful rocks. I stopped at several spots
to take in the views, my favorite of which was the Painted
Wall cliff, with its vivid black and white striations.

TOURING TIP

*If there is a road I particularly like riding, I will often book
a hotel room near the head of that route so that I can travel
on that same stretch at least two days in a row as I explore
nearby areas. I had intentionally stayed in Silverton for
four nights, so that each day I could ride the Million Dollar
Highway as I ventured to other parts of Colorado. As a result,
I was able to ride it eight times this summer alone. Unlike
splurging with dessert, there are no calories associated with
enjoying your favorite routes as often as you would like.*

I also decided to take the East Portal Road down to the
Gunnison River itself, so that I could see the cliffs from the
vantage point below, as well as the river itself up close. One
thing I noticed is that the gorge is so deep that much of the
land along the river lies in shade. I did take a few pictures, but
the deep blue colors of the river and the dark green colors of
the trees, both cloaked in shade, were hard to delineate in the
images. I learned later that there are some parts of the gorge
that receive sunlight only thirty-three minutes a day.

The East Portal Road down to the Gunnison River was perhaps the most precipitous road I have ever ridden and one of the highlights of the day.

I think the highlight of the afternoon was making my way back up from the river along the East Portal's extraordinarily steep and winding road. This road is one of the most precipitous I've been on, and much of the time my bike could not make it into second gear. While I had been to the main part of Black Canyon Park before, I had never ventured past the warning sign to the East Portal Road: "Extreme Grades & Sharp Curves Ahead." The road was not in the best condition, with quite a few potholes. But fortunately, I only saw one other car the entire time, making it possible for me to pick the spots in the road with the most amount of pavement. Making it up such steep terrain on my bike was thrilling, not just because of the incline, but also because it felt so validating to see that I was capable of completing the climb. After exiting the park, I was treated to a herd of wild elk and several deer on my way back to my cabin.

On Tuesday, having thoroughly enjoyed exploring the area around Silverton, I set my sights on Rocky Mountain

National Park. I checked out of my cabin and headed north with my gear to Leadville, stopping in Montrose for a burger at Freddy's and in Gunnison for a delightful, fresh, homemade bread pudding at the Back Country Cafe.

A magical moment—greeted in Leadville, Colorado,
with a double rainbow over a church

Everything about Colorado feels magical to me, and arriving in Leadville for the night was no exception. When I pulled into the gas station there, I was mesmerized by the view of a small country church in a meadow, basking in the sun under a double rainbow. The area had just been hit with strong rain, the land around me was soaked, and the air was unusually crisp and clean. In Leadville, before settling down for the night, I was treated to a spectacular spinach salad with candied walnuts, dried fig, and blue cheese crumbles along with a wood-fired, hand-tossed "carnivore" pizza made with homemade dough at High Mountain Pies. Sitting outdoors on the patio in the sun, savoring my food, and breathing in the fresh mountain air, I couldn't help thinking how full of joy I felt.

The next day I left Leadville for Estes Park, home of the east entrance to Rocky Mountain National Park. I had been lucky enough to snag a timed pass to the park for 3-5 PM the next day and wanted to make sure I was there well in advance. Arriving mid-afternoon, I made a pit stop at Buckles of Estes to have several broken snaps on my chaps repaired, then ordered up a burger topped with bacon and grilled onions as well as hand-cut fries at Penelope's World Famous Burgers & Fries.

TOURING TIP

Most of the time, I believe it is safest to book reservations shortly before arrival. However, if there is a particularly meaningful or significant stop I would like to make, I usually secure reservations about three days in advance and then plan my route accordingly. I also try to make the last leg of the trip the shortest, so that there is an added buffer of time to cover for unexpected problems.

I had a brief scare earlier in the day when I felt a thick bulge under my chin near where my cancer had been located just a few months before. I called Oregon Health and Sciences University and left a message asking my doctor, John Holland, to call me back to discuss whether or not I needed to return to Oregon to have it checked. I was worried I would not be able to reach him, as he was retiring and the following day was his last day at work. He had tried calling me back while I was driving to Estes Park, but at the time, I was navigating hairpin turns on the Peak to Peak Highway and was not able to pull over in time to answer. I was very relieved when he reached me while I was at Penelope's. After asking me about my symptoms, he reassured me that the swelling was a normal reaction to the radiation treatments and should resolve on its own. He was kind enough to ask about my trip and to tell me he might take me up on some of my travel tips as he headed east to visit family. When I hung up the phone, I felt that a weight had been lifted from my shoulders. I was having so much fun on my trip and was incredibly grateful I could continue.

The bike and I both enjoyed the spectacular mountain views from Bear Lake inside Rocky Mountain National Park.

Even though my pass was not good until the following day, the park was open to all visitors after 5 PM, so after eating my late lunch, I headed toward Rocky Mountain National Park. Instead of trying to rush going all the way through the park after hours, I decided to focus that evening's trip on a short side excursion to Bear Lake, inside the park. I started at the Beaver Meadows Entrance Station and followed Bear Lake Road ten miles to the beautiful alpine lake, situated under Hallett Peak and the Continental Divide. The lake was calm and peaceful, with dark, still waters dotted with a variety of boulders and surrounded by V- and U-shaped canyons. I got a great picture of my bike with the mountains behind it, but I think the most delightful part was taking videos of a rafter of wild turkeys as well as three mule deer.

This mule deer at Rocky Mountain National Park seemed interested in showing off his full set of antlers.

The following day I chose to catch up on paperwork at the local library while waiting for my timed slot at Rocky Mountain to open. I went back to Penelope's for lunch, had a chat with the friendly owner, enjoyed another great burger, then headed to the park.

TOURING TIP

My summer trips have always been several weeks long, usually seven to eight weeks. As a result, there are always personal and financial matters that I need to attend to while

I'm away. I often use local libraries to catch up on paperwork, as the computers are typically free. While I can do much of what's needed on my phone, it is helpful to sit down every two to three weeks and make sure everything is in order. For instance, this year I printed out day passes to two national parks. Each summer I also assign someone I trust to collect my mail. Then I call them periodically and ask them to open and read any bills or papers that I can't already access online.

TOURING TIP

If I am in a town for more than one day and find a restaurant that I like, I often return the following day. I know I will have another good meal, and being there more than once allows me to get to know the staff a little better. I love hearing stories about the area and getting local tips, and the restaurants appreciate my repeat business.

I was a little nervous driving to the park, since thunder and lightning were predicted for all of my time window. Because I had booked only a few days prior, the only available time slots were during the afternoon time span, when the Rocky Mountains often experience thunderstorms. However, I decided that I was going to appreciate every minute in the park, regardless of the weather conditions.

Shortly after starting the ascent to the Alpine Visitor Center along Trail Ridge Road, I was, indeed, hit with thunder, lightning, and rain. I chose to stop and enjoy what there was of the view in spite of the rain and met a friendly woman who offered to take my picture. I carry a small, lightweight tripod with me to facilitate getting photos, but with the wind and other weather conditions, it wasn't feasible to use the tripod. She took a picture, and we both went our own way.

I feel most at home when I am near mountains. My grandmother used to joke that my mother must have gone on hikes while she was pregnant with me, because I love climbing uphill. My favorite vacations, other than motorcycle trips, have been the ones I took to visit Grannie in Switzerland. The hike I most adore there is one that involves taking a little mountain train from Nyon to St. Cerque and then hiking all uphill for an hour and half to a small chalet in Gingins for cheese fondue and fresh apple tarts. La Barillette is a primitive restaurant, with toilets sans modern plumbing, but the patio sports a million-dollar view of the French Alps, and the food is divine.

So, while I resolved to enjoy every moment in the Rocky Mountain National Park, I really hoped that at least some of the time there would be without rain so that I could luxuriate in the sun and clearly see the mountains I cherish. When the rain stopped in just fifteen minutes, and the sun broke through to reveal breathtaking views of the Rocky Mountains, I actually cried with happiness.

Reveling in the warm sun and impressive mountain views on
Trail Ridge Road in Rocky Mountain National Park

My ultimate photo opportunity is one that includes my bike and spectacular natural scenery unobstructed by guardrails or cars. Shortly after the rain ceased, I stopped at an overlook with a gorgeous view of the meadows and mountains and pulled into a prime spot right on the edge of the meadow with no cars in my way. The same woman I had met in the rain just a few minutes before just happened to pull into the parking spot across from mine. I recognized both her and her truck and smiled in greeting. She held up her hand to take my phone, saying, "You have to get another shot of you and your bike." The picture she took that day is one of my favorites of the trip, because the smile on my face reflects the absolute joy I felt in that moment—joy that I had survived cancer, a divorce, and the pandemic to make it to this point—reveling in the sheer delight of riding my bike in the mountains, surrounded by spectacular vistas.

Giddy with happiness from the fresh air and invigorating scenery, I pulled into the Alpine Visitor Center parking lot, at 11,796 feet the highest visitor center in the National Park System. I decided to hike up the Alpine Ridge Trail to take in the stunning 360-degree panorama of the Rocky Mountain Range, a trek I had not made before. The hike is commonly referred to as "Huffer's Hill," because the thin air of the high elevation and many steps make it rather taxing, as it rises more than 200 feet in just three tenths of a mile.

There is something about standing at the top of a mountain peak that makes me feel triumphant and generally euphoric. From my viewpoint over 12,000 feet above sea level, I could see the Never Summer Range, Mount Chapin, Mount Chiquita, and the Ypsilon Mountains, along with Trail Ridge Road snaking down below me. The bright sun, strong wind, clean, crisp air, and unparalleled mountain views were exhilarating.

Although the hike was rather short, for me this moment felt climactic. I felt a tangible sense of accomplishment, not just for traveling so far alone on my bike, but also for persevering through the valleys of pain and adversity of the previous few years. During the months and years of hardship, marked by the broken promises that had destroyed my marriage and the physically exhausting cancer treatments,

I'd begun to doubt that I had the fortitude or strength to ever be in a place of joy again.

Even though I walk through the valley of the shadow of death, I will fear no evil, for you are with me; your rod and your staff, they comfort me. (ESV)
—Psalm 23:4, The Holy Bible

As a Christian, I had intellectually believed God's promises to comfort me as I walked "through the valley." But from my low vantage point at the time, I could not see my way through to the other side. Standing at the top of a mountain peak in one of the most beautiful settings in the country, surrounded by mountain meadow grass, deep blue skies, and white-capped mountains, completely alone and yet utterly happy, I had an entirely different perspective.

For several years I had felt isolated and helpless, partially because I was ashamed to admit to others how I was being treated. In addition, I had been fixated on my solution to the problem—saving the marriage—and I was failing miserably at that. After I reached rock bottom and realized that nothing would salvage the relationship, I decided to put all of my life into God's hands. I accepted the fact that I might spend the rest of my years alone and started focusing on how to make the most of my life, with or without a marriage partner.

Facing my deepest fears and choosing to make the most of my life, regardless of the potential difficulties involved, was completely freeing. No longer bound by fears of betrayals, loneliness, or failures, I was now able to focus on what was most important to me—loving others. I became more present with my friends and my children, more energetic with my students, more able to live in the moment, more at peace with myself, more secure in my faith, and more open to pursuing new adventures.

While taking in the magnificent view at the top of the ridge, I reflected on how much joy, unspeakable joy, I was experiencing in that moment. I was content to breathe in the rich mountain air, completely satiated by the mountain views, grateful for all I had experienced on my journey so far, and full of hope for my future. I had literally and figuratively reached new heights of joy.

I took my time going down the mountain to Grand Lake, as I had made lodging reservations just outside the park and there was plenty of daylight left. I wanted to savor every minute of the ride and drink in the beauty of the nature around me. Passing Lake Irene, I saw a gorgeous moose grazing in the meadow to my right and then, just a few minutes later, another one near Timber Creek. The moose were too far away to get a great photo, but in person they were mesmerizing. I have visited all forty-eight contiguous states on a bike and been to numerous national parks, but a moose sighting is still a rather rare occurrence for me, and I certainly had never seen two in one day.

NOTE

My favorite sighting of a moose was several years earlier in Glacier National Park. I had walked to a lake just a quarter mile off a popular hiking trail and happened to arrive at the same time a moose decided to ford the lake. When he first appeared, all I could see was a little brown spot. At first, I thought it was a bear, but as the majestic animal moved forward, its enormous antlers came into full view. Three deer were cavorting in the shallow end of the lake nearby while the sun shone down on all four animals. A photographer nearby had heard of a moose in the area and had been waiting several hours to see it. We were all treated to a close-up moose encounter for at least ten minutes while it crossed the entire span of the lake.

Continuing south on Trail Ridge Road, I was greeted by two separate large herds of elk, grazing on opposite sides of the road in the Harbison Meadows area. I pulled the bike over and ended up spending over an hour taking in the sights before me. What fascinated me most about the elk was the way they seemed to be communicating and interacting with each other. One elk left the herd, turned around, and called to the others. When they did not follow, the elk came back to the group. Mothers were nursing their young, and others were running from one end of the herd to the other. I also saw that I'd underestimated the size of the herd. Many of the elk weren't immediately visible—they seemed perfectly content to lie down in the tall grass, just the tips of their ears showing, flicking back and forth every so often. Quite a few other visitors came and went during this time, and I considered that if I had been traveling with a riding partner they might have wanted to leave. Because I was alone, I could blissfully take in the natural beauty of the wildlife on my own timetable, without being rushed.

The elk herd dynamics were captivating—eating, nursing, calling out to one another, and relaxing in the grass with just the tips of their ears showing.

I exited the park shortly thereafter, picked up some groceries in Grand Lake, then checked in to my hotel nearby and contemplated my next moves. I had booked a room for the next night at the Redstone Inn in Redstone, Colorado, but wasn't sure what route I wanted to take to get there.

I had discovered Redstone by mistake five years earlier. Nestled beneath gigantic red cliffs and consisting mostly of a single main street, it's the kind of place that would be easy to drive past without noticing. The entire tiny village, originally developed by a coal-mining entrepreneur at the turn of the twentieth century to provide housing for his employees, is on the National Register of Historic Places. There is no cell phone service in town and only a few small shops. But the Redstone Inn boasts a grill and fine dining area as well as clean, well-appointed rooms with a rustic décor.

We had first pulled over in Redstone during our cross-country trip five years earlier when my ex-husband suddenly felt sick. Once we realized he would not be able to drive the bike at all for the day, we decided to splurge and treat ourselves to the nicest hotel in town while he recuperated. During the four days we were there, I came to love the food, hiking, and general ambiance of the place. We had visited several times after that on subsequent cross-country trips.

I had mixed feelings about my upcoming stay at the Redstone Inn, since it would be my first time there alone. But I was really looking forward to the nice room and delicious food, as well as the gorgeous scenery I knew I would see along the way.

The most direct route to Redstone from Grand Lake was about 150 miles along a number of beautiful roads, but the ride would take only about three hours, and I knew it would be my last full day to explore Colorado. Since I had not ridden many miles in the previous two days, I decided to take a rather circuitous route to Redstone instead, covering more than double that distance.

The next morning, I headed north to Steamboat Springs and enjoyed a freshly grilled, all-natural burger and homemade onion rings with a touch of chili seasoning at the Backdoor

Grill. From there I decided to go northeast to Walden to visit one of my favorite coffee shops. It was closed, but I feasted on the beautiful scenery instead, leaving room for a great meal later that night. I arrived in Redstone early enough to freshen up for dinner and thoroughly relished my twelve-ounce ribeye steak with gorgonzola herb butter and cheddar au gratin potatoes. The inn was the perfect place to fuel up with food and rest before heading toward the scorching heat of Moab the following day.

Colorado has it all—the view from Granby after
leaving Rocky Mountain National Park.

TOURING TIP

I have learned to travel light on my cross-country trips, packing clothes and accessories versatile enough to allow me to eat out at local burger joints as well as expensive steak houses. Each summer before my trip I splurge on a cute pair of jeans that I really like. Then I plan on wearing those same jeans every day of my trip, freeing up room in my travel bags for accessories that can dress up my look. I pack some

designer sandals, a nice shirt, and some matching jewelry
to complement the jeans, as well as extra makeup for nights
when I will be enjoying fine dining. I keep the need to do
laundry to a minimum by washing the shirt I've worn that
day every night before bed. It is usually dry by morning, but
if it is not, I just attach it to the outside of my bags and let it
air dry when I head out in the morning. A few times during
the trip when a washer and dryer are available, I wear my
shorts and wash the jeans with everything else.

Sitting in the restaurant, satisfied after a long day of riding and a wonderful dinner, I realized that my evening there alone was the best night I had ever spent at the inn. I was proud of myself for facing my fears of being alone and for my willingness to embrace the stay without a companion. It felt almost surreal to reflect on how much joy I had experienced over the last few days. It had been only one month since I had left my home in West Linn, Oregon, yet in a few short weeks I had experienced more treasured, blissful moments than in the previous six years. It was such a relief to have made it through the valley of pain and even possible death, and to have emerged on the other side happier, stronger, more content, and more full of hope than I had ever thought possible.

Elated, proud, and grateful near Capitol Reef National Park after
thriving in triple digit heat on Utah backroads

CHAPTER EIGHT

BE WILLING TO EMBRACE THE HEAT

Days 32–40
Red Stone, Colorado, to Lee Vining, California

I'm not the kind of person who would normally look forward to spending a week riding in temperatures above 100 degrees Fahrenheit. But over dinner at the Redstone Inn, as well as the night before in Grand Lakes, I realized that I had highlighted several national parks on my travel map, all of which were within or in close proximity to Utah. By this point I was feeling stronger and braver, both as a person and as a rider. I wanted to live life to the fullest, even if it required enduring some hardship, so I decided not only to venture out into the heat but to embrace it, learn to relish it, and allow it to teach me more about appreciating my life and the world around me. I ended up visiting seven national parks in as many days and had uniquely wonderful visits at each.

TOURING TIP

I find it adds to the fun and adventure to have a theme for each of my cross-country trips. Previous trips have been about wildlife; friends and family; going from Portland, Oregon, to Portland, Maine; traveling the entire West Coast from the most northwest point of Washington state to the Mexico border and back; and learning to master new roads. This summer my theme was "all of my favorite things." I highlighted the locations of my favorite roads, restaurants, parks, and people to visit and traveled from highlight to highlight.

NOTE

It's difficult to know exactly how many national parks I visited on this ride, as I saw so many. The major parks in order of appearance were Glacier, Yellowstone, Black Canyon of the Gunnison, Rocky Mountain, Arches, Canyonlands, Mesa Verde, Capitol Reef, Bryce, Zion, Grand Canyon, Yosemite, Kings Canyon, Sequoia, and Redwood.

The heat at the Colorado National Monument west of Grand Junction, Colorado, was intense, but the rainbow of colors in the rugged terrain made the visit well worth it.

I left the comfort of the Redstone Inn on Saturday morning and headed west to Grand Junction for a mouthwatering burger and fries, as well as a shot of air conditioning, at Freddy's Frozen Custard & Steakburgers before venturing into Utah. After eating, I soaked my cooling vest, put it on under my leather jacket, and headed toward Colorado National Monument. I entered the park on the east side, near Grand Junction, and then headed west along the historic twenty-three-mile route through sheer-walled canyons, stunning rock formations, and beautiful vistas, exiting near the city of Fruita, close to the Utah border.

Myriad cliffs and sandstone monoliths punctuate the stark landscape of Colorado National Monument's thirty-two square miles.

TOURING TIP

For me, a cooling vest is a must when traveling in exceptionally hot areas, so I keep one in my saddle bag at all times. It is compact and lightweight but makes a world of difference when encountering temperatures in the high 90s or above. The vest lining absorbs water, which then slowly evaporates, cooling me down. To me, it feels like the

*temperature is a good ten to fifteen degrees cooler when
wearing my vest.*

Heading west on Interstate 70 into Utah, the heat was
steadily climbing well into the triple digits, so I decided to
gas up and hydrate at a colorful, alien-themed gas station at
the junction of Interstate 70 and Highway 191 as I headed to
Moab. I spent an hour inside cooling down, drinking water,
and re-soaking my cooling vest while talking with the station
employee. We had a great conversation about biking, and
he gave me a wonderful compliment, asking if he could ride
"bitch" on my bike, meaning riding behind me.

Surrounded by breathtaking sheer red cliffs at Arches National Park

Invigorated by my cooling break, I headed directly
to Arches National Park. It took my breath away. It was as
if the landscape had decided to take a bath in a bucket of
watercolors, with red cliffs, green trees, blue sky, and even an
orange and purple sunset. I was completely mesmerized by
the stark natural beauty of the park and stayed later than I

had intended, simply because I was too spellbound to leave. I took a short hike to view one of the arches and also captured a picture of me on my bike sweltering in the heat with a sheer red cliff towering over me. I was enthralled by the wide range of natural beauty, from lizards running through the brush to one of the most beautiful sunsets I had ever seen—the setting sun beneath the light of a full moon against a backdrop of a rainbow of colors. I made it to Moab in time to have smoked baby back ribs with homemade cheesy potatoes and baked beans at the Blu Pig.

Words can't fully convey the rich hue of colors in this sunset at Arches National Park—from deep reds and oranges to vibrant purples, blues, and greens, this moment in time was breathtaking.

The next morning, I headed north on Highway 191, then southwest on Highway 313 to the Island in the Sky Visitor Center at Canyonlands National Park. The heat was again scorching, but I was able to get water at the visitor center for both myself and my cooling vest. I took a couple quick photos and continued down the road to the Grand View Point Overlook. The overlook provides far-reaching vistas of Island in the Sky, a broad mesa between the Green and Colorado rivers. I was awestruck by the seas of red canyons, mesas, buttes, and rims under the unrelenting onslaught of heat. It was both beautiful and formidable at the same time.

Beautiful yet formidable—red canyons, mesas, buttes, and rims stretching as far as the eye can see in Canyonlands National Park

I intended to go to a Starbucks in Moab for lunch and to cool down. However, when I arrived at the destination on my map app, I realized it was not a sit-down location but a kiosk inside a City Market grocery store with no seating area. Once I got my helmet off, though, I wasn't about to put it back on right away in the heat, so I decided to eat my lunch standing up in the store, next to a table set up with books to read. In an effort to cool down for another long trek in the relentless heat, I stayed at the table for an hour, writing out cards to my children and several good friends. After depositing the cards in the store's outgoing mailbox and using the bathroom to re-wet my cooling vest, I headed south on Highway 191 to the eastern entrance of Canyonlands National Park.

To be honest, the trip to the eastern side of the park was somewhat disconcerting at first. I had expected to see clear signage for the entrance, get information from the park ranger at a kiosk, run into other tourists, walk into the visitor center, get some water, and ask a few questions. Instead, the challenge in visiting this side of the park began almost immediately. For some reason, my map app would not acknowledge the existence of the eastern entrance and kept trying to redirect me north, so I didn't know how far south I would need to keep going to reach my desired point of entry. After over thirty miles in triple-digit heat without seeing a single sign for the park, I began to think I was lost. When I did finally see a sign, it just led me down another long road for thirty-five miles, with no park ranger or manned information kiosk. I finally arrived at the visitor center after traveling over seventy-five miles in searing heat, only to find that it wasn't open and there was no one in sight. I wasn't entirely surprised to find the visitor center closed, as so many parks on my trip had limited their hours of operation due to restrictions associated with COVID-19. It was a little frustrating, though, that the ranger at the northern visitor center had not mentioned the closure that morning and there were no signs anywhere along the entry road indicating the center was not open.

Fortunately, I had obtained a map of the park at the northern entrance earlier, as well as some rudimentary information about the eastern side of park. From my conversation with the ranger that morning, I knew that the two separate entrances were not connected, and if I wanted to see more of the park, I would need to go to the Big Spring Canyon Overlook. The problem was that there was no indication on the map how far it still was to the viewpoint. As I only have a five-gallon tank, I wasn't sure if I had enough gas to get to the overlook and back to Moab. I had seen no gas stations since leaving Moab and no other cars after turning off Highway 191 onto Highway 211 into the park. This would have given me pause in any circumstance, but the heat made the stakes even higher.

I discovered that, although the visitor center was closed, the bathroom was open, and it did have running water, enabling me to fill up multiple water bottles with more drinking water for me and more water for my cooling vest. When I returned to my bike and re-hydrated the vest, some water spilled onto the pipes and instantly turned into steam. I decided to proceed to the overlook, monitoring my mileage and keeping an eye open for other visitors, and I did see three or four other cars, which buoyed my spirits. I also started thinking of my excursion as a pioneering adventure. Traveling through the desolate surroundings in the scorching heat, with no one in sight most of the time, it was easy to imagine I was a new voyager to the area hundreds of years before.

Awe-inspiring views on the eastern side of Canyonlands, almost completely devoid of other visitors

Once I embraced the remoteness and harshness of the environment, I began to see how very awe-inspiring the land around me was. I was opening my eyes to a world very foreign to me—vistas that seemed to go on forever, formidable red cliffs and canyons, and amazing rock formations of every shape and size. Upon reaching Big Spring Canyon Overlook, I could see up close all the beautiful shades of red and brown in the striations of the rock formations. Traveling back toward Highway 191, I marveled at the purple and pink layers in the rock and continued to reflect on how fortunate I was to experience this colorful panorama in solitude. When I finally pulled back onto Highway 191, several hours after first leaving it, I had seen at most ten cars. Upon arriving at the first gas station in Moab, I felt I had not just visited a park, but had completed an epic journey that had tested my resolve and determination. I treated myself to an amazing smoked prime rib dinner back at the Blu Pig before turning in for the night.

The next morning, a Monday, I headed south on Highway 191 and then east on Highway 491 to Durango, Colorado, to have my bike serviced at the dealership there. I had a 2 PM appointment and didn't want to be late, as I hoped to go to Mesa Verde National Park after the bike was serviced. I was in a hurry when I pulled into the ExxonMobil station near the dealership and pulled my handlebars abruptly to the right when a car headed toward me. As might be expected, I dropped the bike.

TOURING TIP

I have found it handy to get to know the service departments at Harley-Davidson dealerships around the country. Over the last six years, I had interacted with the service department at the dealership in Durango at least four times and had been satisfied with their help, so it was good for me to know they were a reliable resource while I was traveling in the Southwest. I had actually been to Durango twice already on this trip, but the first time was during my endurance ride and after the store was closed for the day. The second time was on a Sunday when the dealership also wasn't open. In any case, I hadn't racked up enough miles to need a service on my previous pass-throughs, and the timing was perfect after Moab.

I hadn't dropped the 700-pound bike since shortly after purchasing it, about 30,000 miles earlier, but I knew it was bound to happen sooner or later. Fortunately, I got off easily—I didn't even feel myself hitting the ground, and just a few seconds after falling, the bike and myself were surrounded by at least six guys, who quickly put it upright as I got to my feet. The gas station was located in the same parking lot as an oil and lube service center, and there were numerous employees within a few feet of where I fell who were available to assist me. The men were extremely friendly and helpful, and one of them asked me if I was okay. I replied, "I'm fine, but I'm embarrassed." He laughed and responded with, "You can live with embarrassment." I had to laugh back. Even though I had never been in any danger, I did feel a little jittery. After I gassed up, I was extra cautious about making my way back through the parking lot to the street, not wanting a repeat of my earlier mishap. Despite the incident, I was grateful that the bike was up and I could continue on my way so quickly afterwards.

I did ask the dealership to look for signs of damage or anything out of alignment that might have been caused by the drop. When they gave the bike back to me, they said they didn't see any problems with it. However, about a half-hour after leaving the dealership, I noticed that my right highway peg had been pushed behind the foot control for my rear brake, preventing me from effectively using my rear brakes.

By this time, the dealership was closed, and I really didn't want to take hours out of my day the following day to have them adjust the peg. I decided that this was a perfect opportunity for me to step out of my comfort zone and try to fix the problem myself. Several of my biking friends had suggested I pack hex and Torx socket bit sets, as well as a ratchet and extension, so that I could do minor repairs to my bike on the road if necessary. To be frank, I was proud of myself for packing the tools but hadn't taken time to learn how to use them. When I pulled into Mesa Verde National Park, I tried to adjust the highway peg myself. It took several attempts to figure out, as I didn't even know that I had to move the lever on the ratchet to be able to work the tool the opposite direction. Then it took several more tries to figure out how to loosen and then properly re-tighten the peg securely in the correct spot. I was fortunate that two kind visitors to the park gave me a quick lesson in the use of the tools and worked with me to fix the problem. Even though I ended up needing help to learn how to use my tools, I felt happy and proud that I'd embraced the problem and taken care of it myself, rather than going back to the dealership.

Touring Tip

I do not have locking saddle bags, and I have learned from previous trips that nothing is completely safe if left in the bags when I am away from the bike. I don't want to have to carry my tools in with me every night I stay at a hotel, but I also don't want them easily visible to someone who might open my saddlebags in my absence. I decided on this trip to slide the tools into two different large wool socks and stick one in the bottom of each of my bags. That way, if someone looked in, it would appear as if I had left a sock in my saddlebag. There were only two or three times on the trip where I felt the need to bring the tools inside with me at night. I also keep all essential items for my trip in one saddlebag liner that I always have with me. This liner has my credit cards, cash, riding gloves, medication, goggles, and phone, and when I leave my bike to eat or for any other reason, I take it with me.

Mesa Verde National Park was such a treat. The road through the park to Cliff Palace Loop was full of twists and turns and beautiful canyon views. I saw a bear in a meadow and a coyote carrying its dinner. The most fascinating part of the park was the Ancestral Pueblo cliff dwellings. It is mind boggling that people were able to survive in these villages built beneath overhanging cliffs so long ago. I was able to get close enough to the dwellings to see the individual homes with doors and windows. Since I had arrived in the early evening, I was blessed to see another purple and orange sunset, this time accentuated by the stark black outlines of fire-ravaged trees.

A striking purple and orange sunset accentuated by the remains of fire-ravaged trees in Mesa Verde National Park

The route the next day to Capitol Reef National Park was one of my favorite rides ever, something I would not have thought possible if I had known the riding conditions in advance. I left Cortez, Colorado, and stopped briefly at the site of the Four Corners Monument. It was closed, but leaving from there set me up perfectly to take all small backroads over 200 miles through southern Utah to Torrey. I headed east on Highway 160, north on Highway 41, north again on 162, turned right on Cow Canyon Road, then went north on 191 to Blanding. Blanding was not directly on my way, but I knew it might be a while before I had another chance to hydrate and eat a sit-down meal in an air-conditioned restaurant. The juicy fresh burger and homemade onion rings with fry sauce at the Patio Diner in Blanding were exceptional, as was the service.

From Blanding, I took Highway 95 over 120 miles in brutal heat before I reached Hanksville and could stop for gas. This part of the ride was uniquely wonderful and unsettling at the same time. The rocks and cliffs around me were a stunning bright red and the sky a bright blue, but the heat was in the triple digits, there were no services of any kind anywhere, and I couldn't help wondering what I would do if I broke down.

When I did re-wet my cooling vest, the dripping water again sizzled on my boiling hot bike. I passed only a few cars going the other direction, and the one motorist I saw going my way was a biker who appeared to be in trouble. His bike was pulled over, his helmet was down on the ground behind his back wheel, and he was sitting under some bushes. I had recently learned that this helmet placement was the international sign for a biker in distress, so I stopped to see if he was okay. He said he was just resting in the shade, so I continued on my way.

I ended up getting one of my favorite bike photos ever, when the state route passed directly through a carved opening in a large, bright red cliff. With no traffic for miles, I parked right on the road and got an amazing photo of the bike surrounded by sheer walls of flaming red.

Driving through the stark landscape with no sign of habitation, it was easy to imagine being an explorer many years ago, surveying the rugged land. I have an incredible admiration for the native populations who made it their home. As I rode, it was almost as if time stood still. I savored every moment of the heat and the beauty, grateful that I could take it all in on my own.

I stopped at Natural Bridges National Monument on my way north. Again, the visitor center was closed due to the pandemic, and I could not find any available information on the park, but I was able to take a loop through the monument, get some pictures of the beautiful natural bridges, and enjoy the vistas of layered rock. I saw little wildlife except for a single deer and couldn't help wondering how it survived in the heat.

It didn't surprise me to learn later that all the buildings in Natural Bridges Monument area are solar-powered.

One of my favorite shots of the summer—the bike engulfed on both sides by nearly vertical red cliffs on the backroads of Southern Utah

I gassed up and hydrated in Hanksville and continued west for about fifty miles on Highway 24 toward Torrey through Capitol Reef National Park. One of the wonderful things about this park is that so many beautiful vistas can be enjoyed without even leaving the highway. I marveled at the expansive views of this 100-mile wrinkle in the earth, appreciating the many colorful layers of sandstone, canyons, and rock formations. I stopped for gas right before Torrey and was able to get a great picture of me with my bike in front of a rainbow-colored panorama—blue sky; orange, purple, sage green, and red layers of rock; and green brush. The look on my face was one of elation, both from having survived and thrived in the heat and from experiencing the ride of a lifetime.

My accommodations that night at Capitol Reef Inn and Cafe were perfect: a reasonably priced room with delicious food on the same property. The chef prepared a wonderful southwest chicken salad with charred corn, black beans, avocado, and house dressing.

I left Torrey the next morning, intending to see Bryce Canyon National Park and call it another wonderful day. I had no idea that I would end up visiting yet another national park that would completely steal my heart.

Help! This was one of the last frames I captured before jumping off the bike and running the opposite direction. Fortunately, the farmer's herding dog diverted these cows at the last minute before they ran over the bike.

I took backroads south from Torrey and soon encountered my first adventure of the morning. A large herd of cattle was coming down the middle of the road in Kingston, Utah, and I wasn't sure how to avoid them. I thought they wanted to go right, so I moved to the middle of the road, but then they shifted to the left. They all had beautiful solid white coats, and I stopped to get a video, but without any warning, they turned again and headed straight for me. I had to stop filming and abandon the bike momentarily to get out of the way. Then, out of nowhere, a little cattle dog ran up beside the cows and efficiently herded them off to the side of the road. I love the way my video ends with the cattle coming right at me. These unexpected and unique surprises are of one of the reasons I so much enjoy cross-country travel, even while facing a cow stampede!

I continued south to Panguitch on Highway 89, then east on Highway 12 to Bryce Canyon, known for its statuesque rock formations called "hoodoos." There is a veritable ocean of these fantastic light red structures visible at several overlooks in Bryce. I stopped several times to take in the sights, but my favorite spot was Inspiration Point. It is at a slightly higher elevation than some of the other viewpoints and has a really spectacular view across the sea of orange.

I left Bryce Canyon around 3:30 in the afternoon and anticipated driving straight to my hotel. Having never visited Zion National Park before, I had booked a room in Springdale, thinking I would use it as my launching pad for a visit to Zion the following day. I realized something was up right around the time I hit Mount Carmel. I was only twenty-eight miles from the hotel, but my map app indicated it would take me forty-nine minutes to get there. I hadn't looked closely at the map and didn't realize I would be driving straight through Zion to get to my lodging for the night!

The minute I entered Zion, I was enthralled. To me, it felt like a biker's dream come true—immaculate roads, tight twists and turns, and magnificent views. The transformation of the landscape is immediate when entering the park. The road becomes a reddish-brown color and has almost no tar snakes or potholes. The rock formations change shape entirely, and they seem to be in perpetual motion. Rolling hills, swooping dips and curves, swirling mounds, stark steep cliffs, and pointed outcroppings—topography that made it seem as if someone had dipped a paint brush in orange and gone wild with abandon. As if that wasn't enough, the park also features a tunnel over a mile long. When it was completed in 1930, the Zion-Mount Carmel tunnel was the longest in the United States. After exiting the tunnel, motorists are greeted by several glorious hairpin turns on the way down into Springdale.

I had driven through Utah on a bike several times but for some reason never visited this magnificent national park. I was too captivated my first time through this national treasure to do more than gawk at the sights. I took a couple of pictures and slowly drank in the surroundings as I completed the route to Springdale.

Falling in love with Zion National Park's pristine roads and sensational variety of red- and orange-colored rock formations

Heading east through the park toward the Grand Canyon the next day, I decided to take my time capturing the experience in photos and videos. I got a 360-degree video of towering red cliffs surrounding me near Canyon Junction, several photos of the varied swoops and swirls in the topography, pictures of the reddish-colored road with orange cliffs in the background, and another one of my favorite shots of the summer—the bike and me in front of a backdrop of at least three different types of orange rock formations.

I couldn't get enough of the swoops, swirls, and spikes of red in Zion.

Reaching the east entrance of the park, I realized I wasn't ready to leave, so I turned the bike around and decided to go back and forth without stopping for pictures at all. As I savored my ride through the park, I reflected on how lucky I was that I had decided to embrace the heat of southern Utah.

My next stop was Kanab, Utah, my launching off point for the North Rim of the Grand Canyon. I booked my stay there for two nights, as I knew it would take me a while to get to and from the Grand Canyon the following day.

The North Rim was not at all what I had expected. I had visited the South Rim several times in my previous cross-country trips. Its stunning vistas of multi-colored layers of rock, impressive geological history, and easy access from major cities attract millions of visitors every year.

Enthralling! The dramatic display of colors on Cape Royal Road on the North rim of the Grand Canyon is picture postcard perfect.

Imagine my surprise when I arrived at the entrance to the North Rim, saw only one other car in front of me, and almost got run over by a herd of buffalo! The herd rushed from their meadow across the road in front of me and then, before the dust even settled, rushed back again. I pulled over to catch my breath and take some photos but was a little leery of staying so close to the herd for very long.

I drove directly to Grand Canyon Lodge, ate lunch, and hiked the Bright Angel Point paved trail to a spectacular view of the South Rim of the canyon. From there, I rode the twisting and turning Cape Royal Road over twenty miles through the Kaibab and Walhalla Plateaus, stopping at several overlooks along the way. It was almost surreal to see such amazing natural beauty in the absence of crowds and tour buses.

Learning to embrace the change in scenery in Cane Beds, Arizona, after leaving Kanab, Utah, behind and heading towards Tonopah, Nevada

I left Kanab, Utah for Tonopah, Nevada, the next morning. I wanted to make good headway toward Yosemite National Park but knew to get there I had to brave the heat near Death Valley, the hottest and driest place in North America. My original strategy for dealing with the sweltering heat was to stop as few times as necessary for gas that day to minimize my overall time on the bike. However, after eating lunch in St. George and heading south on Highway 15, I witnessed a thirty-mile, stop-and-go traffic back-up going the other direction. There wasn't a single bike among all those motorists, and I started thinking about how much hotter I would be if I couldn't move quickly. So I ditched the original plan and decided to add a hydration and re-fueling stop to my itinerary.

I pulled over at a Love's Travel Stop just before Las Vegas, only about a hundred miles from St. George. A pickup truck with several guys in it pulled in right behind me, and I struck up a conversation with one of them. Somehow we ended up trading cancer stories. It turned out that he had also had throat cancer but had to have a significant portion of his tongue removed, as evidenced by the large scar on his throat and the way he spoke. It was a sobering reminder of the magnitude of my battle. I was truly touched that a complete stranger took the time to share his story and was so positive about me and my trip.

I didn't take any selfies that day as I traveled over 400 miles in triple-digit heat past Death Valley on my way to Tonopah. Instead, I focused on hydrating, driving safely, and celebrating the uniqueness of the desert topography. At first glance, there didn't seem to be much to see. There was no shade of any kind for much of the trip, and the vegetation seemed to include only patches of sparse brown grass on top of mounds of dirt. However, looking closer, I could see how beautiful the brown really was. There was green-brown, yellow-brown, orange-brown, gray-brown, black-brown, and of course, dark brown-brown. It was a great reminder about how much beauty we can see in the world around us if we look closely enough.

For some reason, perhaps the heat, I had seen almost no motorcyclists since leaving Colorado eight days earlier, but when I pulled into the parking lot of my hotel in Tonopah, I encountered a large group of bikers traveling from California to the legendary Sturgis Rally in South Dakota. It was fun to hear about their adventures as a group, see their different bikes, and share road trip stories before we parted ways and traveled in opposite directions. I had been to Sturgis several weeks before and was heading to California the next day.

My Sunday trip from Tonopah to Lee Vining, California, was one of the most delightful rides I have ever been on. I headed west on Highway 6 and then took Highway 120 into Lee Vining. The air was a little cooler, and I could see an interesting silver-blue body of water to my right through the trees. It turned out that Lee Vining is home to Mono Lake, over a million years old with "tufa towers." These calcium carbonate spire and knob formations are caused by the interaction between the salty lake water and freshwater streams. The prettiest feature is the lake's startling silver-gray-blue-colored water.

The startling silver-gray-blue-colored water of Mono Lake stood in stark contrast to the deserts of Nevada the day before.

The most amazing part of this day turned out to be the road itself. About forty miles before Lee Vining, on Highway 120, I saw the first indication of the treat awaiting me—a sign warning of dips for the next five miles. What followed was mile after mile of glorious ups and downs in the road. The dips were numerous and varied, and many were huge, taller than the bike and impossible to see over. It was as if the guy in charge of leveling the road was on vacation when they made this one! I would bomb up a hill, get a brief moment of weightlessness, then swoop down the other side, only to be met by another dip. I felt like a kid in a candy store and was having so much fun I was whooping, laughing, and chortling out loud. It was much better than any amusement park ride I've ever been on.

One of the highlights of the trip—gravity-defying dips
on highway 120 east of Lee Vining in California

I got to Lee Vining in time for lunch and took the afternoon to explore Tioga Pass, just outside the east entrance to Yosemite National Park, as well as Mono Lake. The pass features beautiful mountain views, as well as picture perfect sights of Tioga Lake and Ellery Lake. Despite the breathtaking scenery, however, I couldn't get my mind off how much fun I had had on Highway 120 earlier in the day.

In the six years before this trip, I had experienced more pain than I had ever thought possible. One of the lasting blessings born from that hardship is the extent to which I now appreciate living life to the fullest and enjoying every moment. So, while I knew other people might think it strange to leave the magnificent views at Tioga Pass and drive over eighty miles round trip just to enjoy some dips in the road, it made all the sense in the world to me. As I drove east toward the road I had already been on earlier in the day to experience the dips again, it felt so freeing to know that I could choose joy, choose adventure, and choose happiness, no matter how it appeared to anybody else.

A sign of the natural wonders yet to come—
just outside Yosemite National Park

Captivated by the splendid lake views east of Yosemite

I also realized that the desert had taught me that there can be beauty in the midst of hardship, blessing in the midst of pain. The scorching heat of the last week had been significant, but it had also given me a better appreciation for the stunning beauty around me. Choosing to take on the challenge of the triple-digit temperatures and learning to thrive in such a foreign environment also gave me more confidence in my ability to overcome obstacles in general. I could have picked a cooler part of the country to explore, but flourishing in Utah had made me feel stronger as a person, more confident about trying new things, and more optimistic about the positive future God had in store for me.

On Tioga Pass, excited about finally returning to
Yosemite for the first time since childhood

In many ways, the lessons I was learning on the road were reinforcing how I was stretching and growing as a person overall. My counselor had explained to me in the early spring, before leaving on my trip, that I could heal more as an individual if I could become grateful for the pain my ex-husband had caused me. To me, that seemed like a stretch. It is one thing to acknowledge that good can come out of bad—that was doable. But to be grateful for the hurt in the first place, particularly when it means someone you loved and trusted violated that trust in more ways than you could have imagined? I wasn't sure how to get to that point but told my counselor I would work on it. I thought that perhaps I could practice by becoming more grateful for hardships in general.

Almost immediately, I had the opportunity to put my therapist's advice into practice when the pandemic hit and the high school that I had taught at for over twelve years shifted to comprehensive distance learning (CDL). I find my job immensely rewarding. In fact, when I walk through the doors in the morning, I do not feel like I am coming to work. I am invigorated by the back-and-forth interaction with so many young people and find it meaningful to make a difference in the lives of the next generation.

The switch to CDL came with many challenges— learning to put paper and electronic documents into PDF form, modifying curriculum for the changed course parameters, communicating by video rather than in person, and providing significant feedback electronically rather than on paper or in class. However, after a short while it became obvious that CDL would be our learning model for quite some time. Rather than focus on the difficulties presenting themselves, the longer work hours, and the numerous changes required, I decided to frame my months in CDL as an opportunity. How could I use this time to grow as a person, learn new skills, and think of creative solutions to important problems?

During the period of CDL, I learned to set up and host Zoom sessions, create a Google Classroom, produce math videos, set up my own YouTube Channel for the videos, utilize an iPad to upload and comment on electronic versions of student tests, and access important school documents and programs from home. Although all of these skills will be useful and valuable resources to draw upon in future years, it is unlikely I would have learned many of them if we hadn't had to switch to distance learning. I am grateful to have been placed in a challenging circumstance that gave me an opportunity to grow as a teaching professional.

My resolve to learn to be grateful for hardships was significantly strengthened by my time in the Southwest. Remembering the beauty I encountered in the midst of heat, as well as my ability to be an overcomer in a harsh yet stunning environment, gave me confidence that I can use the same determination and positive outlook to learn and grow from current difficulties.

A room with a view—the tents in Curry Village at Yosemite National Park may have been primitive, but the setting was unparalleled.

CHAPTER NINE

CELEBRATING ROOTS IS IMPORTANT TOO

Days 41–51
Lee Vining, California, to Bend, Oregon

Although I am now happily settled in Oregon, I lived in California for almost half of my life. From birth to age thirteen, I lived in several Bay Area cities, and for fourteen years of marriage and motherhood I lived in Southern California. Although some of my childhood was challenging, I have many fond memories of the California Coast, as well as positive impressions from past experiences of Yosemite National Park and Sequoia National Park. When I was a little girl, I used to love going to the beach with my family for the day. My mother would cook delicious snacks like sausages and let me run up and down the beach eating and playing. After helping us children rinse the sand out of our swimsuits, she and my father would take us to dinner at a Chinese restaurant, then dress us in our pajamas and let us fall asleep in the car on the way home. My father had introduced us to Yosemite and Sequoia during camping trips, and I still remember loving the smell of the trees and the freshness of the air. I had not returned to either Yosemite or Sequoia since my pre-teen years and had always wanted to go back, but none of my previous adult traveling companions had ever wanted to visit there with me.

So it had been with a sense of determination that I had highlighted Yosemite National Park on my traveling map, making it one of the top priorities of the summer. During my travels in Utah, though, my plans to visit Yosemite hit a speed bump. I discovered that due to COVID-19 concerns, there were a limited number of day passes available to enter the park and that all of the passes for the month of August were sold out. Fortunately, I further researched the park's travel restrictions on my phone and discovered that visitors with overnight reservations in the park were allowed in both the day of their reservation and the following day.

Still, my problems were not over, as none of my booking apps listed any available lodging within the park. After fruitlessly searching for a couple hours, I called my friend, Grant, and he helped me figure out that I needed to look on the Yosemite National Park's reservation site. Even there I could only find one spot left—a tent at Curry Village. I had no camping supplies with me, but the tent did come with bedding, and I decided to make the reservation so I could enjoy the park.

Driving into Yosemite that morning felt like a victory celebration. I was so grateful to finally return to the park and to be able to appreciate its natural beauty through the eyes of an adult. I traveled west on Tioga Road, pulled over at one of the first entrances to Tenaya Lake, hiked a short distance to the lake itself, and enjoyed a picnic lunch while soaking in the view of the gorgeous blue waters and surrounding mountains. After a friendly conversation with two other visitors, I continued west to Olmsted Point, glimpsing my first view of Half Dome. Wow!

This view of Half Dome from Yosemite's Olmsted Point was one of three park highlights recommended by the ranger at the entrance station.

Seeing the stunning, distinctly-shaped granite rock formation made me understand why so many people come to Yosemite every year. The incongruity of the sheer rock face on one side and the smooth and round shape on all other sides is strikingly unique. I have seen many different mountains in my life but never anything quite like the dome in Yosemite. It was refreshing and inspiring to spend time taking in the vista and getting a variety of pictures.

Next, I continued through the park until reaching Curry Village in Yosemite Valley. Located beneath Glacier Point and near the base of Half Dome, the accommodations at Curry Village boast a five-star view. I had originally planned to check in and then drive elsewhere in the park, but when I saw how beautiful it was in the village itself, I decided to just spend the evening there, relaxing and taking in the scenery. Many usual services, including some dining options, were not available during the pandemic, but I was quite happy to look up at the mountains and trees, both from my tent and from the food carts nearby.

My neighbors in the tent next door recounted that a bear had walked through my tent site a few days before. Even though I placed all of my food and anything that had a scent in the bear storage at the campsite, I was still a little nervous about going to sleep that night. I envisioned how little protection my canvas tent walls would provide against the sharp claws of a bear.

A once-in-a-lifetime shot of Half Dome at
Glacier Point in Yosemite National Park

The highlight of the park was my trip the next morning to Glacier Point. Although the park was at reduced capacity, there were still quite a few visitors in Curry Village and the surrounding areas, so I breathed a sigh of relief when I saw the warning sign at the beginning of the road to Glacier Point: "No trailers or vehicles longer than 30 feet." I knew this was a good indicator that tight curves and switchbacks were coming up, so traffic would be greatly reduced. The road did not disappoint!

After several miles of twists and turns, I was rewarded with a spectacular view of Half Dome, Yosemite Valley, and the Sierra Nevada mountain range from an even higher vantage point than the night before. I was able to get yet another favorite photo of summer—me sitting high on a rock, surrounded by glorious mountains, white clouds, and blue sky.

I had encountered an unexpected dilemma the week before. Two of my very best friends had invited me to stay at their houses along my route on the way home to West Linn. If they had asked a couple months before, I would have accepted the invitations immediately, but as I traveled across the country on my own, I was experiencing a new sense of empowerment and freedom that came with no longer being afraid of being alone. I was enjoying my solitude so much that I wasn't initially sure if I wanted to switch gears and be more social. Upon reflection, I realized that I couldn't think of anything more important than showing these dear friends how grateful I was to have them in my life and called both Kathy Nesper and Michelle Martin to give them my approximate windows of arrival time. I planned to stay with Kathy in California right after leaving Yosemite and with Michelle a week later in Oregon.

So leaving Yosemite, I headed south on Highway 41 to Fresno and from there went to visit my friend, Kathy, and her husband, DW, at their home in Tulare, California. Kathy and I had met twenty-four years earlier when we both worked on a public relations campaign designed to educate families concerning widely distributed misinformation about child development. I admire Kathy because of her integrity, compassion for others, wisdom, and faithfulness. She is super tech savvy and has helped me out of more than one technology crisis. Kathy was also one of four friends who had come to spend time with me in Oregon immediately after my recent divorce.

During the last several years, I had socialized less than usual, primarily because of the stress related to my failing marriage.

The pain from the marriage difficulties had been exhausting. Sometimes after devoting so much of my energy to my work and children, I just hadn't felt that I had the strength to get together with friends. As Kathy, DW, and I gorged on home-baked pizza and salad that evening, we laughed, shared stories, and encouraged each other. It was a relief to be in such a healthy place emotionally and to be able to fully enjoy the camaraderie.

The next day Kathy and I headed to Sequoia National Park, with me on my bike and her in her car. I wanted to maintain a safe distance during the pandemic and also didn't want to miss out on all the curves on my bike. Our first stop at Hume Lake Christian Conference Center for lunch was delightful. We enjoyed delicious hot dogs from the Hume Lake Snack Shop, and she shared memories from her many visits to the center over the years.

After eating, we took Ten Mile Road out of the conference center to Generals Highway. Any thoughts I had of enjoying a relaxing ride after a nice meal were quickly banished, as this back route seemed to have more potholes than there were trees in the park. The fact that many of the pits were cloaked in shade made them difficult to see and travel rather precarious. Not mere divots in the road, these gaps seemed at times big enough to get lost in. Passing one notable hole, marked with a red warning cone, I could not see the bottom. However, I quickly shifted gears, focusing on safe driving, and to thinking about what an adventure the trip was.

Although I hadn't been to Sequoia since I was a child, I still had vivid memories of the enormous trees in the park. The woods had always felt welcoming to me. My childhood was sometimes stressful, but whenever I was in the forest I felt at home. I enjoyed breathing the fresh air, feeling the cool shade, and smelling the wonderful woodsy fragrance, so it was a special treat to revisit this natural paradise. As we drove south on Generals Highway to the site of the General Sherman Tree, I savored the vistas at various overlooks and breathed in the fresh forested air.

The giant sequoias were magnificent—as large as a car at the base and taller than the eye can see when looking up. They took my breath away. On the walking path down to the General Sherman Tree, I passed through two giant twin trees that survived a fire and grew right next to each other. They were so tall and grand that I didn't feel a regular photo could do them justice, and I asked Kathy to take a video, starting with me between the bases of the trees and going up to the top of the tree line. My presence in the clip, as well as the length of the video itself, helped to convey to a certain extent how very tall the trees were.

Just a short walk from the twin trees, we were treated to a close-up encounter with the General Sherman Tree, by volume the largest tree in the world. We walked around the tree, gazing up at it but couldn't really grasp its enormity. It is over 100 feet around the base and over 270 feet high. The first branch of the tree is a whopping 130 feet off the ground, taller than the total height of most

Dwarfed by the majestic General Sherman Tree at Sequoia National Park

other trees. I asked Kathy to take a panoramic picture of me in front of this tree, as it was also really impossible to capture the essence of it in a regular photograph.

After we had our fill of the giant trees, we headed south on Generals Highway through the park. That segment of the drive alone would have made for a spectacular day. There were numerous hairpin turns with million-dollar views of the valley. Once on flat land again, we headed west on Highway 198 and then north on 99 to Kingsburg for dinner at Roadhouse 99. This self-proclaimed "old school" bar and grill is located in a nondescript building but offered an amazing bacon cheeseburger and homemade onion rings. Famished from the technical riding late in the day, I devoured every onion ring on my plate.

As I headed west to the San Francisco Bay Area the next morning, I felt rejuvenated and refreshed from my time with friends and the visit in the woods. I was so glad I had made it a priority to celebrate my friendship with Kathy and her husband, as well as to rekindle my love for the giant trees.

My destination that day was Conzelman Road in the Marin Headlands, just north of San Francisco. I had done the road by car several years earlier with my cousin and older son and again the previous year on my bike. It is one of my top five favorite rides in the country. For me it has the perfect trifecta for bikers: immaculate road conditions, spectacular vistas, and a hair-raising course. There are actually two separate loops to Conzelman Road. My goal that day was to hit the one that goes from just north of the Golden Gate Bridge, up to Hawk Hill, and then over to Bonita Lighthouse.

I hoped to do the road before dinner and then meet up for the evening with my best friend from junior high, Michelle Levin. Michelle and I both attended Redwood Middle School in Saratoga in the late 1970s and had become reacquainted the previous summer. We had been very close in junior high but had lost touch with each other after I moved to Oregon before the beginning of ninth grade.

From Tulare, I headed north on Highway 99, then west on Highway 152 to Gilroy, stopping to eat at the In-N-Out Burger, one of my favorite options in the western states. There were memories for me in Gilroy as well, since I had lived there from the late-'60s to the mid-'70s. I remember the town as being largely agricultural, with garlic fields everywhere. We used to drive past them with our windows open, smelling the garlic. While Gilroy is still the garlic capital of the world and the wonderful fragrance persists in the area, it has been greatly developed since I left.

I went north from Gilroy, driving through the city of San Francisco and over the Golden Gate Bridge. My family lived in San Francisco for several years, and I never got tired of seeing the glorious, "international orange," almost two-mile suspension bridge over the blue waters where the bay meets the ocean. I couldn't have had a better trip across the narrow straight to my hotel in Mill Valley—the sun was shining, the winds were mild, and there was none of the summer fog that is common in San Francisco.

My room at the Muir Woods Lodge in Mill Valley, just four miles from the Golden Gate Bridge, was perfectly situated for my route up Conzelman Road. After grabbing some snacks and checking into the hotel, I headed south on Highway 101, got off at exit 442, took two quick turns, then turned left onto Bunker Road. The famous one-way, mile-long tunnel on Bunker Road is a fun way to begin this adventurous route. From there I turned left on McCullough Road, then took the next exit on the roundabout up Conzelman Road to Hawk Hill.

What a spectacular vista! From Hawk Hill, the view encompasses the entire northern San Francisco skyline, the Pacific Ocean, and the Golden Gate Bridge. As a biker, though, my very favorite part is the section of road right after Hawk Hill—a one-way drive with a cautionary sign regarding the eighteen-percent grade: "Warning. Cyclists Use Extreme Caution. Steep and Winding Road Ahead. CHECK YOUR SPEED." Passing the sign and heading down the hill feels like dropping off into space. There is a sense of weightlessness, and the road seems to continue right into the ocean. It is absolutely thrilling! Needless to say, I was glad I had gotten new brakes in Durango, Colorado.

Proof of the thrilling ride to come on the Conzelman Road in the Marin Headlands near San Francisco

Having navigated the steep grade and winding curves, I followed the road until it ended at the Point Bonita Lighthouse trailhead. I was hoping to get a picture of me with my bike in front of the Golden Gate Bridge without any obstructions. There had been photo opportunities at Hawk Hill, but a railing at the top of the cliff there partially blocked the view of the bridge. The picture was particularly important to me, as the location felt significant. I had memories of the Bay Area as a child and of my visits there as a wife. But this time at the Golden

Gate Bridge I was completely alone and also completely happy. The area was familiar to me, but my growing sense of confidence and inner strength was completely new.

I parked in the lot at the beginning of the trail to the still-active 1855 lighthouse and was surveying the area to find a good angle to take a picture when I struck up a conversation with a gentleman parked next to me. Once he realized what kind of photo I was hoping to get, he started directing the shoot. He asked me to drive my bike along a section of dirt and up onto a walking path, and then turn it pointing downhill. Then he told me how to sit on the bike and what to do with my helmet. After a few minutes of listening to and following his animated advice, I was not surprised to find out that he was a photographer by trade. He ended up getting a great shot of me and the bike in the sun with the bay and the Golden Gate Bridge behind us. What a blessing and a treat! I was so grateful for the unexpected kindness and generosity of a stranger, not to mention the great weather. It had been foggy all week before the day I arrived.

An eye-catching gift from a stranger—an unobstructed picture of the bike and me in front of the Golden Gate Bridge

After soaking up a few more rays of sun and some more glorious views of the bay, I headed back toward Highway 101 to visit my friend, Michelle Levin, in Corte Madera. As friends in junior high, we spent many weekends together at her dad's house in Santa Cruz. That time with Michelle at the beach had been positive and rejuvenating. Although Michelle and I had spoken briefly the previous summer, we had not seen each other since the late-'80s. She did not yet know about my cancer battle or my divorce.

I was grateful that Michelle had made time to see me at a moment's notice, as I didn't know until shortly before I arrived exactly when I would be available. It was wonderful to see her that evening, meet some of her family, catch up on her life, and talk about my year. I was amazed how easily the conversation flowed. To me, it didn't seem that she had aged at all, and it felt completely natural to share. Michelle has always been so gracious, kind, and perceptive.

It is interesting how sharing with someone who knows your history and who is also perceptive can provide new insights into your own life. During our conversation, Michelle empathized with me over my extensive cancer fight a few months earlier. It was true the battle had been brutal. The daily radiation and several rounds of chemo took their toll on me physically. It was difficult being in so much pain, struggling to eat or drink, not being able to speak, and living with the anxiety of not knowing if the cancer would kill me before I even had a chance to see grandchildren.

Talking with Michelle, however, I realized I was actually grateful for the cancer. I was happier than I had ever been, primarily because having cancer had forced me to re-evaluate my life and make changes I might not have had the courage to make otherwise. I had known for months that my marriage was most likely not going to last and that the dynamics were unhealthy for me and my children. But I kept holding on, hoping we could somehow salvage it.

Once I knew there was a good possibility I might not be around much longer, I decided I wanted however many months I had left on this earth to be as positive as possible. To that point, whether or not to divorce had been a murky decision in my mind, a choice that was never quite definitive. But with the prospect of a greatly shortened lifespan looming on the horizon, my path became much clearer. When I finally did make the decision, I was so relieved and determined to see it through that I actually ended up filing on the way to the emergency room. I was on my way to the courthouse when the nurse on my cancer team at Oregon Health and Sciences University returned my call from the night before. I had left a message explaining that I had a fever, a potentially serious warning sign for someone battling cancer. She was adamant that I needed to be admitted immediately and said she would call ahead so they would be waiting for me. I knew I might be hospitalized for a few days, so I decided to take the fifteen-minute detour to file before going to the hospital. I knew that taking care of my emotional needs would give me greater strength to face whatever physical battles came next.

My close call with death also had given me the strength to make other helpful, life-changing choices. After making the decision to leave one toxic relationship, I realized there were other relationships in my life that never should have lasted as long as they had. As with my marriage, I had held onto these connections longer than I should have, partially out of a desire to please others and partially because I felt some kind of responsibility to maintain the bond. It was so incredibly freeing to realize that I didn't have to allow toxicity of any kind into my life. It was okay to let these harmful relationships go and instead to choose to surround myself with positive, faithful, kind, and loyal friends.

Facing death head on also had given me the courage I needed to embark on my eight-week, solo cross-country trip. Yes, I was worried about traveling alone and how I might face potential problems that could come up on such a long trip.

But what could be worse than suffering from the lies and betrayals in my marriage and then finding out I might die from throat cancer?

Ultimately, I felt I had been given a second chance at life, one that I didn't want to waste. While talking with Michelle, it had been over six weeks since I had left Oregon, and I had loved every bit of it. Not only was I having the time of my life riding every day, exploring the country, and meeting wonderful people, but I was also growing more confident, hopeful, and strong as a person. So, when Michelle expressed sympathy over my cancer ordeal, I surprised myself when I was able to honestly tell her I was so glad to have gone through the trial. Without even realizing it, I was learning to do exactly what my counselor had suggested would be so very healing— feeling grateful for a significantly painful event in my life.

An up-close shot of an amazing engineering feat—the Golden Gate Bridge as seen from Battery Spencer

The next morning I planned to head north on Highway 1 up the California Coast, but before I did, I wanted to explore Conzelman Road again, this time on the loop that leads to

Battery Spencer. After going through the tunnel on Bunker Road, I took the second exit on the McCullough Road roundabout and went back toward the Golden Gate Bridge to the Battery, built in the early 1900s. After a short walk along the Battery, I was treated to one of my very favorite views of the Golden Gate Bridge. From the vantage point of the Battery, the northern end of the bridge looms larger than life. I was able to get a great picture of the bridge with San Francisco in the background before heading back to my bike.

Once on my bike, with Hawk Hill just up the road, I realized I wasn't ready to leave yet. I simply couldn't resist going back around and doing the same loop up Hawk Hill and down the steep, one-way road along the ocean that I had done the night before. I was having so much fun that I decided to do it two more times. I had the giddy feeling of getting off a really awesome roller coaster ride and not being able to refrain from running back to the end of line to do it all over again—except there was no line, just glorious sun, the blue water, and an open road.

A bird's eye view of San Francisco taken from Hawk Hill on
Conzelman Road in the Marin Headlands

After getting my fill of Conzelman, I turned north on Highway 1 to Stinson Beach. I had eaten at the Parkside Cafe there last year and hoped they would be open again. I was in luck. I dined on some of the best fish tacos I have ever had— slightly crispy fresh fish with a light, yet flavorful sauce and a nice side salad. Invigorated by the success of the morning, I also helped myself to two desserts to go.

The ride up the coastline was beautiful and rejuvenating. I planned to spend the night in Gualala, California, as I was looking forward to eating at Upper Crust Pizzeria. I had ordered a small pizza from there to share the previous summer without realizing how delicious it would be. I had spent all year wishing I had ordered a larger one and looking forward to eating there again. Unfortunately, right after I checked into my hotel and started walking over to the pizza place, the power in the entire town was shut off. Apparently, there were rolling blackouts in the area, but no one I spoke with had known this one was coming. Since all of the businesses were shutting down and there was nowhere to get dinner, I had to improvise. I got a small side salad to go from the pizza place, added my own hard-boiled egg, and ate it back at the hotel, using the light on my phone to illuminate my room.

Since I couldn't go to dinner, I decided to spend some time that evening at the beach instead. The Gualala Bluff Top Trail was immediately across from my hotel, and there was just barely enough time left for me to walk over to the beach, sit down, and enjoy watching the orange and yellow sunset on the Pacific Ocean.

I stayed in Gualala longer than originally planned the next day, simply because I didn't want to leave without getting my pizza. After checking out of my hotel, I walked around the little town, enjoyed the view of the ocean, and explored the farmer's market. I was the first person in line when the pizza place opened and got an entire meat lovers pizza just for myself. It was worth the wait!

The power may have gone out in Gualala before Upper Crust Pizzeria
could make my pizza, but I drank in the light show put on
by Mother Nature instead.

From Gualala, I headed north along the coast again,
not really sure where I would end up that night. I find the
coastline so therapeutic and inspiring and just wanted to
enjoy the day without a set plan in mind. I pulled over at Van
Damme State Park and relaxed on the beach there, finishing a
good book and eating my leftover pizza. It was so restful and
peaceful to lean against a large piece of driftwood, feel the
sand with my toes, and watch children playing with shovels,
couples kayaking on the water, and seagulls parading around
the seaweed strewn on the beach. Afterward, I got back on the
road to continue north.

One of the things I loved about this section of coastline
was the many places where the road was covered with trees.
Even on the coast, the temperature was up to 100 degrees as I
headed north, and the shade provided a welcome respite from
the heat as well as a freshness to the air. During the first part
of my journey north from Gualala, I was often surrounded by

the wonderful fragrance of eucalyptus trees. Farther north I could smell the redwoods.

One of a variety of refreshing canopies of shade trees on
Highway 1, north of Gualala, California

I stayed in Garberville that night and left the next morning for the Avenue of the Giants. The large redwoods were magnificent, and I enjoyed taking several photos. A friend had recommended a route that would take me west through Humboldt Redwoods State Park and then hug the shoreline on backroads through the towns of Honeydew, Petrolia, and Ferndale. I loved the idea of getting as close to the ocean as possible and seeing a part of California I had never been to.

I had a fun day, although I must say I felt like a contestant on the *American Ninja Warrior* show who didn't quite make it to the final bell. The ride started off great, with so many hairpin turns that my GPS map app looked like an earthquake high on the Richter scale. The turns themselves weren't a problem—a road like that can be an exciting challenge. But the condition of the road rapidly deteriorated, with open potholes and patched up potholes covering much of my path.

I encountered gravel and dirt and one-way lanes with signs warning to "proceed when clear" but could not see around the curves to know when the road was indeed unobstructed. The most unique challenge was a one-way bridge made out of wood that wasn't firmly nailed down. I bounced my way across the narrow, raised slats, praying none of the loose boards was sticking up enough to catch my wheel.

Lush greenery, fresh air, and smooth roads provide an inviting welcome to Humboldt Redwoods State Park.

I was feeling fairly confident having made it that far and was hoping to complete the loop when I encountered a steep downhill dirt road littered with lemon-sized rocks. I was sitting there trying to convince myself I could make it down the hill when a large truck came from behind me and fishtailed down the slippery slope. Seeing that, I finally realized I had to turn around. The good news was that by going back the way I had come, I knew what to expect. Also, when I got to the state park that I had driven though earlier in the day, I realized I still had plenty of time to explore, so I went on short little hiking trails to the "Tall Tree," "Giant Tree," and "Flatiron

Tree." I still laugh thinking about the challenges of that day. I don't have a desire to try the road again, at least on my Harley, but it did add a little spice to my trip.

Narrow slats and loose boards on the bridge at Honeydew, one of many obstacles on the way to town from Humboldt Redwoods State Park

The next day I went north toward Brookings, Oregon. There is a pancake house there that I love, and I wanted to make sure to be in town the next morning for breakfast. It was amazing how much cooler the coastal weather became as I got closer to Oregon, an almost fifty-degree differential from Honeydew. I drove through Redwood National Park and enjoyed the various groves and majestic trees. My favorite was a tree called the "Corkscrew" Tree. Apparently, there is debate about whether it is a cathedral tree or several trees that grew around another one that subsequently died. I took a video of its entire length to try to capture the essence of it on film. Near the entrance to the park there was a huge herd, or gang, of elk lounging in a meadow next to a motel appropriately called "Elk Meadows Cabins."

Do these elk realize they are camped in a meadow next to a sign that says "Elk Meadows Cabins?"

After leaving the park, I stopped at Trees of Mystery. I'm not really the type to do tourist-type things, but this place was pretty cool. I took a four-tenths-mile hike winding around a variety of trees with labels like "Upside Down Tree," "Elephant Tree," and "Brotherhood Tree." I also took a tram up through the tops of the trees to what would have been a great view of the ocean if it hadn't been too foggy to see much of anything. It was a nice change in perspective to be up so high in the trees after walking through the bottoms of them for days.

When I arrived at my hotel in Brookings and unpacked my things, I noticed a problem with the bed. As I had driven up earlier, the sign out front said "new bedding" and "clean rooms." However, when I pulled back the cover of my bed, I noticed short and long black hairs all over the pillow and sheets! I called the owner of the hotel, and she insisted the bed was clean but that the maid must have lost a few hairs while she was making it. The owner was not rude to me, but it was a little disconcerting that she didn't believe me when I said the bed was dirty. I tried explaining that there were also black flecks on the sheets, and there was no way the linens were clean. She still didn't agree with me but offered to give me a new room. However, I was worried the maid might have "lost hairs" in the new room also, so I asked for clean sheets with the intention of re-making the bed myself and staying put.

A welcome respite from the heat at the fog-enshrouded coastline near Brookings, Oregon

The owner did not want to come into my room because of concerns with COVID but brought sheets to me and stood outside the door watching while I changed the bed. As I stripped the linens off the bed, a used bandage fell out of the old sheets. I screamed, and the owner finally admitted that the bed was not okay. I decided there was no way another room could be worse than the first one, so I moved all of my belongings. She ended up "comping" me the room, and I was happy that I ended up with a free night's stay. I must say, though, that I don't intend to reserve a room there in the future.

The next morning, a Tuesday, I had a delightful breakfast at Mattie's Pancake House. Mattie's is one of those old-fashioned pancake houses that keep things simple and tasty. They use fresh local ingredients and cook each meal to order. The waitresses are friendly and treat diners like family. I had some delicious strawberry crepes and bacon to fortify me for the trip that day.

A quintessential picture of Southern Oregon farmlands in Lakeview on the way to Bend—a familiar and welcome change of pace after days on the coast

After breakfast, I headed east from Brookings and rode over 300 miles to Lakeview, Oregon. My plan was to visit another Michelle the following day in Bend—this time Michelle Martin, my best friend since high school. We have been fortunate to live relatively close to each other for the last forty years and have supported each other through many of life's ups and downs. She is one of the kindest, smartest, most compassionate people I know. I admire how she parents her children and also handles the curve balls life has thrown her. I can share anything with her and know she will always be there for me. She had texted me earlier in my trip to see if I could stay at her house in Bend on my way home, and I was very much looking forward to relaxing with her, catching up on how her summer had been, and sharing photos of my trip.

Rather than going straight to Bend from Brookings on Tuesday, I decided to use the extra day to explore more of southern Oregon first. I had arranged to spend Wednesday and Thursday night with Michelle and thought I could use the extra time to go to Lakeview, as I had never been there before. I had spent much of the previous five summers sightseeing in all forty-eight contiguous states but realized there were parts of my home state that were still new to me.

I traveled over 300 miles east through Grants Pass, Medford, and Klamath Falls, stopping in Grants Pass for an In-N-Out Burger. I absolutely love their double-double, animal style, protein-style burgers. It was delightful to just bomb down the road that day with no planned stops, glide through the curves, and take in the views along the way. I think my favorite part of the route was from Klamath Falls to Lakeview. The temperature was more moderate, and it was such a treat to see the farmland after being on the coast for most of the last week. I passed a fire that had been burning for several days, but the town I was staying in was not in danger.

On Wednesday, I headed north from Lakeview toward Bend, stopping in La Pine for lunch. As I was parking my bike, an elderly lady got out of a pickup truck and started a conversation with me. She was very enthusiastic about me traveling alone and ended up sitting outside at the table next to mine for lunch. At the end of my meal, the waitress told me I didn't have to pay. It turned out that my sweet neighbor had taken care of the bill for me.

My next stop was the Harley-Davidson dealership in Bend. I wanted them to tighten a loose part, and while I was there I asked them to put on new tires for me. The service people were friendly, helpful, and informative. I left the bike at the dealership and got a ride from Michelle back to her house.

There has always been an easy familiarity between Michelle and me. For some reason, we always seem to laugh a lot when we are together. I think part of it is that both of us have had to deal with some significant challenges in life. We enjoy living in the moment, celebrating what that day has to offer, and making the most of our time with each other. In high school in Bend, we were both straight-A students by day and pranksters by night. One time we toilet-papered a friend's yard so thoroughly that his dad woke up and thought it had snowed. On another occasion, we found some abandoned street signs on the side of the road and used them to decorate another acquaintance's property. A friendly policeman later admonished us for re-purposing the signs but must have laughed it off as harmless childhood antics because he did not ticket us.

To me, the focus of this leg of my trip was primarily on celebrating my roots by visiting places in California that had held meaning to me over the years and spending time with friends I had known since my younger days. I had found comfort in the woods, enjoying the large trees, exploring the coast, and connecting with people who had been there for me in the past. It had also given me time to reflect and think about the formative experiences of my life. What I was starting to realize was that, while these roots were part of what created who I was today, they did not necessarily define who I was today. I could not change the realities of my early years, the fact I had gone through two divorces, or that I had battled throat cancer. However, I understood now that it was completely up to me how I would choose to respond to those events.

Embarking on this solo cross-country journey was a choice I made, not only to celebrate life but also to prove to myself that I could use the difficulties I had endured to become stronger, more confident, and more capable than ever before. Although the places I visited and people I spent time with in California were familiar to me, I was not the same person I had been when visiting them in the past. For the first time in years, I was making significant life decisions based on confidence, not fear.

So when I walked into Michelle's house that night to set my bags down, it felt known and new to me at the same. It was comforting to be somewhere I felt loved and accepted and also exciting to know that I was in a better place than ever before to appreciate it. Both Michelle and her daughter commented that evening that I must be tired from all of my travels. I was surprised and happy to tell them that I didn't feel tired at all. In fact, the traveling had completely rejuvenated and relaxed me.

Spending time with Michelle over the next two days was absolutely delightful. That night we went to Jackson's Corner and gorged on their "honey pie" pizza, made with fennel sausage, marinara sauce, mascarpone cheese, jalapeños, and honey. The restaurant makes their pizza dough every day, hand tosses it, and bakes it in a fire brick oven. It was wonderful to talk and laugh and enjoy such good food together.

The next day, Michelle and I got inner tubes and floated down the Deschutes River in the sun. It was so fun relaxing, talking, enjoying the water, and appreciating the views together. Michelle is always so calm, even when action needs to be taken immediately. One time in high school in Bend, when I was driving Michelle somewhere, I neglected to see a stop sign coming my way. At the very last moment Michelle said, "Are you going to stop?" Fortunately, thanks to her comment, I did. This summer on the river, we were so busy talking and having fun that neither of us noticed the warning signs instructing floaters to disembark on the left. At the very last moment, Michelle said, "Oh, by the way, we need to get to the other side so we don't go down the rapids." We both started laughing and giggling, while madly paddling with our hands to safety.

That night, as I packed up my gear in preparation for leaving the next day, I was filled with a sense of joy and hope for my future. Just the year before, I had felt so overwhelmed by life's challenges that I had sometimes wished I didn't need to wake up in the morning. Yet only months later, I was thoroughly enjoying myself on a solo, eight-week, cross-country trip and giggling like a high-schooler with my best friend.

Giggling like schoolgirls on the Deschutes River in Bend, Oregon

My conversations with friends over the last several days had been enlightening. While recounting stories from years before with them, I had come to realize that my past hardships had made an impact on me but did not have to direct my future. Acknowledging and celebrating my roots had given me an opportunity to reflect and learn. With my inner strength and growing confidence, I could now move forward in my life with a sense of hope and purpose.

Stopping to appreciate the red, yellow, and black bands of clay at the
Painted Hills Monument near Mitchell, Oregon

CHAPTER TEN

LIVE LIFE WITHOUT REGRETS

Days 52–55
Bend, Oregon, to Creswell, Oregon

I had originally planned to return home from my cross-country adventure on August 24, the night before my teaching job resumed, but our school district decided to delay the beginning of the school year by one week. I called my daughter to ask if she would mind if I came home a day late, since that would be exactly eight weeks from the day I had left. As usual, her advice was wise beyond her years. She said, "Mom, honestly, one day won't make a big difference to me. It's more important that you have no regrets about your trip when you get back."

Her comment was both freeing and thought provoking. I was happy that I could round out the trip to exactly eight weeks. It also prompted me to pose a question to myself:

"How can I end this journey having no regrets?" The first thing I decided was that I wanted to see more places in my home state that I had not yet visited, places I couldn't easily get to on a regular weekend.

So when I left my friend Michelle's house on Friday, my plan was to head east to the Painted Hills. I had seen pictures of these glorious bright red rolling hills taken by colleagues who had traveled during the summer and was shocked to learn the unusual natural beauties were right in Oregon. The topography was nothing like what I could see near my home area in West Linn.

What a glorious day! My first stop on Highway 26 was in Mitchell, a small town situated just a few miles from the Painted Hills Unit of the John Day Fossil Beds National Monument. I gassed up at the town pump, enjoyed a juicy burger from Tiger Town Brewing Co., and purchased a thick slice of freshly made banana nut bread from Painted Hills Pastry. The pastry was exceptionally moist and flavorful, a pleasant surprise for me, as I have a much harder time tasting baked goods now than before my cancer treatments.

After hydrating and filling up my water bottles, I headed a little less than ten miles west to the entrance of the Painted Hills. Since the road up to Painted Hills Overlook is gravel, I decided to park the bike and hike up to the viewpoint, not wanting a repeat of my Honeydew adventure, where loose rocks and gravel had forced me to turn around.

The trek was more than worth it. At the overlook, I had a 360-degree view of gently sloping, multi-layered hills of all sizes and shapes. The hills are made up of bands of clay, "painted" in many different shades of red, yellow, and black. Apparently, these differently colored streaks and spots reflect the differing temperatures at the times the clay was deposited. I was able to get some beautiful pictures, as well as a video of the panorama all around me.

The 360-degree view of exquisitely colored striped hills at Painted Hills Monument was worth the final trek by foot on a gravel road.

Rich farmlands heading east on US Route 26 through farmland in Mount Vernon, Oregon, on the way to Baker City

A striking, surreal view of fire-damaged trees on the desolate mountain tops of Oregon Route 245 leading into Baker City

From the Painted Hills, I headed east on US Route 26 through beautiful farmlands and fields of green and yellow, dotted by freshly baled hay. I decided to take the back way to Baker City, and instead of going from Highway 26 to Oregon Route 7, I went via Oregon Route 245. In some ways, this last stretch was my favorite part of the day. I loved the way the road twisted and turned through the mountaintops with almost no signs of civilization. I only saw one car on the entire forty-mile stretch, and that was at the very end. It also felt rather surreal, because there was still smoke in the air from a recent fire and much of the landscape was rather stark. I was surrounded by gray, ashy hills covered with burnt trees. A few deer ran into the road at one point, and I narrowly avoided dumping my bike as I braked hard to avoid hitting them. This landscape felt worlds away from the Painted Hills earlier in the day and at the same time uniquely captivating in its own right.

I spent the night in Baker City, in anticipation of heading to Hells Canyon National Recreation Area the next morning.

This area was also on my bucket list for Oregon—I had heard of it from many other bikers but had never been there myself.

A riveting perspective of the winding road on the edge of the cliffs above the Snake River at Hells Canyon

Hells Canyon was everything the name conjures up—hot and dry, with brittle grass. At the same time, it was also blue and green and cool where the Snake River wound through the gorge at the bottom. To me, the canyon seemed all about these sharp contrasts—deep canyons beneath tall mountain peaks and parched landscape surrounding a lush river. The canyon is the deepest river-carved gorge in North America. The road winds and curves right along the edge of the gorge all the way to the dam. At the dam, I took a brief break to hydrate and share my map with another motorcyclist who was lost, since the visitor center was closed.

Heading west back toward Baker City, I had not yet figured out where to spend the night. I was so glad I had decided to visit places in Oregon that were new to me. Yet at the same time, I felt a sense of sadness overtaking me with the realization that my trip was coming to a close. My daughter's words echoed in my head, and I wondered what the best way would be to end my trip.

This concrete gravity dam on the Snake River in Hells Canyon along the Idaho and Oregon border is 1,680 feet above sea level and the largest privately owned hydroelectric power complex in the nation.

I wanted its impact to extend beyond the vacation itself. I realized that I was becoming a stronger and more confident person, and I wanted to have time to reflect about what I had really learned during my adventure. I also had toyed with the idea of writing a book about my journey and wanted time to ponder what I might say to encourage or inspire others. I knew from my two endurance rides earlier in the trip that traveling long sections of road at a time created a perfect opportunity to reflect more deeply and evaluate where I stood in life and where I wanted to be.

So, as I arrived back in Baker City around five o'clock Saturday evening, I decided I wanted to go an additional 1,500 miles by Monday night, leaving me a whole day to enjoy the Oregon Coast before heading home on Tuesday. After pulling into a gas station, I got out my map to see what my options might be. I also called my friend, Grant, to bounce ideas off him. When he heard what I wanted to do, he said, "I don't think you have enough time." I laughed and said, "Grant, I've traveled over 1,500 miles in a day and a half twice this summer already. I think I can make it." I had thought about going north to Canada, but the borders there were closed to all except essential personnel due to the COVID-19 pandemic. Then I noticed a perfect triangle—Baker City to Salt Lake City to Reno, then back to Oregon. It would be about sixty miles short but otherwise fit the bill perfectly.

I gassed up my bike, chugged a protein drink, and headed for Salt Lake City around 5:30 PM on August 22. The minute I started heading east on Interstate 84, my spirits lifted. It felt empowering to know that I had it in me to travel almost 500 more miles after an already full day of riding. It was also absolutely wonderful to bomb down the road, follow the flow of traffic, and not worry about stopping for anything other than gas. My mind was free to think about all the things I had learned on my trip so far and all that I had to be grateful for.

I realized as I drove down Interstate 84 that I had learned a different lesson on each segment of my summer trip. Traveling from Oregon to Custer, South Dakota, I had discovered that I would never really feel alone. Successfully completing the endurance ride from Custer to Niagara Falls helped me see that I was stronger than I knew. Visiting my son in Washington, DC, after not seeing him for so long, made me realize I was blessed beyond measure. Effectively dealing with the mechanical issues in DC, traveling so far on the Blue Ridge Parkway on gravel, and then successfully riding Tail of the Dragon twice gave me confidence in my abilities, not only as a biker in my own right, but also as a woman.

As I outran thunderstorms in the Southeast, completed another endurance ride to Silverton, and overcame the unexpected challenge of sharing my hotel room with a young man who was a stranger, I had determined that I would not let obstacles stand in my way. While riding the Million Dollar

Highway and exploring the mountains of Colorado, I knew that I had literally and figuratively reached new heights of joy in my life. My decision to embrace the heat of the Southwest and open myself to all that it had to offer taught me the benefits of being grateful for difficulties. Taking the time to explore my roots in California and spend time with friends helped me realize that I could make a choice to grow from my past experiences and chart a new course for the future. Being intentional about how to spend the last few days of my trip reaffirmed the value of living life with no regrets.

All these thoughts flowed freely into my head as I swiftly headed east, stopping in Boise, Heyburn, and Tremonton for gas. I arrived at my hotel room in Salt Lake City around 1 AM. After briefly texting both Grant and Kathy to let them know I had arrived safely for the night, I got out a piece of paper and drew a diagram of the key segments of my trip, with a brief description of key inspirational discoveries for each. It was clear that there was a book within me waiting to be put to pen.

As I left Salt Lake City for Reno on Sunday, I had a renewed sense of hope and purpose. My summer ride was coming to an end, but the lessons I had learned along the way would benefit me for the rest of my life. I stopped for gas in Wells, Battle Mountain, Lovelock, and Sparks. After grabbing a quick bite to eat in Sparks, I decided to pass through Reno and head north again before settling in for the night in Susanville, California. I had covered about 600 miles that day.

Much of the trip since Baker City had been through smoke, as wildfires ravaged much of the region. When I pulled into Susanville, it was somewhat alarming to see actual flames rising into the air very close to my hotel. In the morning, my bike was covered with ash, and I passed numerous fire trucks on my way north out of town.

I took backroads northwest from Susanville to Interstate 5 and then continued north to Creswell, Oregon, arriving Monday evening after almost 400 miles of riding for the day. My voice was hoarse from two days of riding through smoke, but I was so glad I had put on the extra miles. I had a renewed sense of hope about my future, had fleshed out the main ideas I wanted to put in a book, and had thought through how to make the last day of my trip particularly meaningful.

I was grateful my daughter had spurred me to think about the importance of living life without regrets and was happy I had taken the time to reflect on how to use the lessons learned on my trip to live life more fully. With these thoughts settled, I could turn eagerly toward home.

Reunion with the twins after a life-changing solo,
eight-week, cross country trip across the US

CHAPTER ELEVEN

A HOMECOMING WITH HOPE

Day 56
Creswell, Oregon, to West Linn, Oregon

I woke up on Tuesday, August 25, excited about my last day on the road. The time would be filled with many of my favorite routes and stops in Oregon, starting with breakfast at the Creswell Bakery. I had discovered this food destination by accident several years earlier, when heading south to Medford from West Linn. Located just outside of Eugene, the bakery makes all of its menu items fresh every day, uses local ingredients, and creates every meal to order. They even raise their own cows for the beef in the sandwiches and smoke their own bacon. I ordered the ciabatta bacon breakfast sandwich and slathered extra butter on the bun. That morning was not a time for worrying about calories.

Whenever possible, I like to take the back way from Creswell to the Oregon Coast, so just two blocks from the bakery, I turned left onto Oregon Avenue, which quickly becomes Camas Swale Road. After about nine miles, I turned right onto Territorial Highway and then took Oregon Route 126 west all the way to Florence. There are a lot of tight turns, green trees, fresh air, gorgeous views of the Siuslaw River, and little in the way of traffic. Every time I do it, I find the ride fun and relaxing at the same time.

I gassed up in Florence and then headed north along US Route 101 toward Newport. This fifty-mile stretch of 101 is one of my favorite sections of Oregon coastline, since it is so close to the water the whole time and the view through the trees is so pretty. There are many curves, and the road is in good condition. I passed through Yachats, Waldport, and Seal Rock on my way to the Pig 'N Pancake in Newport.

It is my annual tradition to end my summer road trip at a Pig 'N Pancake on the coast, and this year was no exception. I ordered fresh strawberry crepes with whipped cream and a side of bacon, drenching my bacon with maple syrup and the crepes with marionberry syrup.

After heartily enjoying my second full meal of the day, I drove to Otter Crest Loop. This short loop is such an adventurous way to see the coast, because it is a one-way road most of the route, the pavement hugs the cliffs, the speed limit is low, and there is hardly any traffic. The views are breathtaking and easy to appreciate from multiple overlook points. I felt so fortunate that the sun was shining, and I was able to stop and get some great pictures of myself, the bike, and the ocean to commemorate my trip.

Finishing up the Otter Crest Loop, I felt that my adventure was complete. I had seen my son in DC, completed two endurance rides, driven over 15,000 miles, hit almost all my favorite destinations, discovered new territory, eaten many delightful meals, met so many kind people, and explored numerous glorious natural wonders.

Now my thoughts turned toward home and my two beautiful twins waiting to join me for dinner upon my return. It had been eight weeks since I had left, but those weeks had contained enough memorable moments to last a lifetime. More importantly, I had proved to myself that there was hope beyond cancer and a second divorce. Single or not, I had a renewed sense of optimism about my future.

A fitting way to end the trip—a sun-drenched view of the coast from Otter Crest Loop, an adventurous, winding, one-way road that hugs the cliffs near Newport, Oregon

Back in Oregon after eight weeks on the road—although it might have seemed like the end of the trip, in many ways it was just the beginning.

CHAPTER TWELVE

WHERE THE RUBBER MEETS THE ROAD

Day 57 and Beyond
West Linn, Oregon

It's always a little crazy when I first return to West Linn from my summer cross-country trip. I stay on top of things back at home as much as possible while I am away, but house and yard work always build up over my absence. I wrote up a to-do list when I got back that filled more than a full single-spaced page.

One of my biggest priorities was re-connecting with my two children at home, both of whom were entering their sophomore year in college and doing distance learning because of the pandemic. My daughter would be taking her classes from our house in West Linn, while my son would soon be joining his friends to do distance learning in an apartment near campus, two hours from our house.

Shortly after my return, the twins and I went blackberry and flower picking at a nearby farm. On the ride back home, I shared my ideas about the book I wanted to write, animatedly describing my adventures, how happy I was, and what I had learned.

I very much appreciate that all of my three children are now old enough to give me great advice. I have learned to listen to it! As my younger son was listening to me talk about the book, he said, "Mom, what's the climax? I mean, a book needs to have an ending that makes the story worth reading."

As these chapters have shared, I had changed as a person during my summer journey. Just a few months before, I had felt a deep sense of hopelessness and wondered if I would ever be happy again. I had wracked my brain trying to find a way out of the pit of despair and saw no light in the distance. I was exhausted from trying to be cheerful around my students, colleagues, and children while enduring such deep emotional pain.

A large stumbling block for me had been my fear of being alone and my general lack of self-worth. I knew my marriage was unhealthy but was afraid to end it. I didn't want to be on my own, and I was afraid I would be ashamed of myself if I divorced a second time.

My close call with death gave me the courage to do what I ultimately knew I needed to do, but that was only the beginning. I needed to learn to practice gratitude on a daily basis, draw upon my faith for strength, learn to travel on my bike on my own, take comfort in good friends, and also make new ones.

My two-wheeled cross-country trip was just the "wind therapy" I needed. Throughout the journey, I developed new heights of confidence, joy, and hope. I now find that I am happier than I ever thought possible. I have and always will have various tribulations, but I am confident now that I can approach them with strength, learn from them, and continue to live a full and blessed life.

I realize now that I had completely misunderstood how God sees me. Where I was fixated on my mistakes and failures, He was focusing on the character He wanted to develop in me. Where I saw defeat and despair, He saw forgiveness and hope. Where I saw shame, God saw a beautiful daughter whom he loved.

So what is the climax of this book for me? It isn't really about me—it's about the reader. From the beginning of my thoughts about a book, I felt compelled to write one that might inspire and encourage others. I felt a palpable sense of relief when I finally faced my fears and followed through on healthy choices to turn my life around. But doing so was probably the hardest thing I've ever had to walk through.

I hope that others reading this book also will be inspired to follow their dreams and not let fear rob them of their joy. I firmly believe God has a hope and a purpose for all of us and cares about both our small and big dreams.

Some readers have a desire to ride a motorcycle but are afraid to get their endorsement. Take the first step and then the next one! Others already ride and aspire to take a solo trip but are frightened of being alone. Get out the map and start dreaming! Let your passion for the ride give you the determination you need to pursue the trip of a lifetime. Many are stuck in difficult life situations with no apparent hope in sight. Ask yourself, "What choice would I make if fear were not a factor?" Then ask for the strength to make that change! Others feel a calling to take on a challenge, to accomplish something new and significant, but are uncertain if they would succeed. Try anyway! It's better to have tried and failed then never to have given yourself a chance.

You are not alone! Time after time on my summer trip I experienced the inherent and abundant kindness of others. As I traveled through twenty-eight states, complete strangers gave me traveling tips, helped when I was lost, offered to take my picture, shared their life stories with me, and affirmed me and my choices. From the hotel reservationist who gave me a ten-percent discount for being "bad ass," to the Harley dealerships who serviced my bike quickly and got me back on the road, and to the property manager who found room for me when I didn't want to spend another night sharing my bunkbed with a stranger, these fellow Americans consistently demonstrated generosity and compassion. And of course, I believe that God was my guide and fellow traveler from start to finish. I was traveling on my own—but never alone.

Basking in the sun on the California coastline, realizing that the past
may have shaped me but did not have to define me. God's
promise for me is a future and a hope—and that
hope is available for the reader as well.

In my classroom after the trip, so full of joy that a
colleague describes a "sparkle" in my face

AFTERWORD

After returning from my cross-country journey, I realized I had a rather significant decision to make—would I merely look back on my summer adventure with fond memories, or would I choose to use the experience to genuinely reshape myself? Put more simply, would there be a "happy ending" that truly lasted?

While it is impossible to know exactly what the future holds, I am delighted to report that well after the end of my trip, I continue to experience an abiding sense of inner confidence, joy, and hope.

Where does this positive perspective come from? Part of it is from being in a place of emotional health after so many years of excruciating pain and hardship. My friends mention that before my divorce they could see how anxious and strained I was, not just from their conversations with me but also from the pallor of my face and my tense expression.

They tell me today my face is more open and happy, my color has improved (probably partly because my cancer treatment is now further in the past), and I appear more vibrant, even "ebullient" or with a "sparkle." My son Ethan notes, "Now, when we have a conversation, it's wonderful to see your eyes light up whenever you talk about a past or upcoming trip."

Another basis for the joy welling up in me is my newfound freedom from fear in general, so much of which is due to the lessons I learned from my trip. Facing fears and overcoming obstacles throughout my adventure has given me a sense of confidence and inner strength. One colleague tells me that it shows even in the way I walk and talk.

My initial focus after cancer and divorce was finding a riding companion for a summer journey. I knew a cross-country adventure would be restorative but was afraid of traveling alone for eight weeks and tackling on my own any problems that came up while on the bike.

Some of the pivotal conversations I've described in this book helped me shift my focus from concern that I couldn't do a trip alone to considering how I could accomplish it. My thoughts turned from the impossibilities of solo travel to the logistics of traveling safely on my own and preparing myself mentally.

Leaving on the adventure required faith that somehow I would learn what I needed to along the way and the courage to follow through on that faith. But the most impactful stage of my transformation was the journey itself. The obstacles I conquered became visible reminders of what I had overcome, as well as a reassurance to me that God was always with me. My friend, Michelle Martin, who knows me well, affirms, "You became more self-sufficient, more God-sufficient. The Lord was riding shotgun with you. You were not alone."

Successfully reaching so many milestones on my trip demonstrated to me that I could indeed do what I set out to do, giving me confidence to see the world from a position of strength and hope rather than fear. My transformation from *can't* to *how* became *did*. My daughter Eleanor notes, "You proved to yourself a lot of things you needed to prove."

Experiencing triumphs on my trip also helped me to go through the next important stage of my personal journey toward a place of confidence, joy, and hope—learning to see myself as a person of value again. I had felt like a failure after the end of my marriage, focusing on the mistakes I had made, my inability to solve the problems, and all of the negative repercussions that my children and I had experienced as a result. I doubted my worth after years of being betrayed and privately and publicly belittled.

Taking on such a challenging motorcycle trip, accomplishing so many of the important goals I had for the journey, and having so many positive interactions with other people has helped me to see myself as a person of value once again. I realize that my worries of living a life of shame after a second divorce were groundless, that God does indeed have a future and a hope for me.

Looking back on my journey now gives me an enduring tangible reminder of what I have learned. When facing new difficulties and feeling overwhelmed, I now often ask myself, "Kathleen, what did you learn in Utah?" As a result, I am less afraid of obstacles, knowing that I am in a place of strength to deal with them. My son, Elliot, has encouraged me by noticing that I now deal with stressful situations with more clarity of mind and positivity.

Embarking on the trip itself solo was also definitive in that I took ownership of my love for motorcycling—it wasn't a hobby that my husband and I were doing together anymore, but a passion that I could now own in my own right. I am a biker, with or without a riding partner.

My perception of myself and the world I live in has changed. No longer controlled by fear, I am free to experience a joy I never thought possible. I am confident in my strength and hopeful about my future. As my son, Ethan, pointed out, I am excited about life.

Life will always be full of uncertainty. But I am a different person now than I was before my trip. And that is, indeed, a happy ending.

ACKNOWLEDGMENTS

I've always wondered why an author's acknowledgements are often so lengthy. Now that I've actually had the honor of writing my own book, I understand why—it takes the support, advice, encouragement, and wisdom of friends and associates from all corners of our lives to breathe a book into being. As with any birthing process, I had no idea what I was getting into ahead of time—and that's probably a good thing!

First of all, I would like to thank Road Dog Publications for being willing to take a chance on an unknown author. Mike Fitterling was kind enough to respond to my initial enquiry about submitting a manuscript when I emailed him from Colorado, halfway through my summer 2020 trip. His considerate and informative response gave me the confidence and direction I needed to keep my dreams of the book alive.

Secondly, I would like to thank all three of my beautiful children, of whom I am so proud. It was my love for you that kept me from giving up when my difficulties seemed insurmountable. Thank you for loving me enough to support me in my passion for riding, even while knowing the inherent dangers associated with such a way of life. Eleanor—I so much enjoyed and appreciated our almost nightly check-ins on the road. Elliot—I am so grateful to you for manning the home front while I was gone. Ethan—thank you for not only giving me a compelling reason to cross the country on my own but also welcoming me with open arms when I arrived.

Grant Myers and Leo Guzman Fernandez—you were two of the first Rose City HOG members to invite me on group rides when I first started looking for biking partners. Your encouragement, assistance, companionship, and confidence in my riding abilities helped give me the wings I needed to fly solo.

Kathy Nesper—it's safe to say you were uniquely instrumental in making this book possible. You checked in with me nightly on the road, found gas stations for me on my second endurance ride, helped with the editing of this book, and even directed me in finding and setting up a replacement computer when my old one crashed shortly after I submitted my manuscript.

Michelle Martin—your unwavering friendship through all life's storms over the last forty years has sustained me in the hardest of times. Thank you also for making your home a haven for me before, during, and after my trip.

Don Weber, Kathleen and Roger Bufford, and Diana and Atwood Lynn—your faith in my ability to ride solo across the country and your encouragement to follow my dreams were a much-needed push in the right direction at just the right time.

Barb Edwards and Suzie Q Holm—you led the SouthLake Church Bible Study that helped me to realize I am never really alone. That blessed assurance was the foundation upon which my trip was laid.

Jena Starkes—I knew within one minute of working with you that I was going to love you. You've got all the brains, technical know-how, and patience I could ever hope for in a web designer and general right-hand woman.

Rose City HOG—your support, affirmation, and acceptance make me feel like a part of your family. Paul Gooch—I so much appreciate your sage advice on the road, especially your admonition to "take your time in Utah." Mike Webb—thank you for urging me to bring my own tools and also providing me with timely tips on the trip. Jenni Cramer—I'm so glad you introduced me to the IBA. Waldo Wollrabe—your suggestions for gaining an endorsement were invaluable.

NRJKG—you know who you are. None of us could have predicted the twists and turns we would experience together over the last three decades. I'm so grateful to have had your advice and abiding friendship through every challenge and endeavor, including this book.

To my colleagues at West Linn High School—your overwhelming display of encouragement, affirmation, and support throughout my struggle with cancer helped me overcome many challenges and see strength in myself I didn't even know I had. I especially appreciate Tina Laferriere for being the first person to urge me to write a book about my journey.

Michelle Levin—I'm so glad we reconnected. I appreciated your thought-provoking questions and comments this summer, as well as the referral for the outstanding literary lawyer.

Stephan Mantanovic—thank you for helping me to negotiate and finalize such an equitable and appropriate publishing contract.

Jean Davidson—I am so grateful to you for reading my manuscript and endorsing my book. I admire you so much as a businesswoman, author, and head of the non-profit children's safety program called "Yell and Tell," which is spreading around the world. I hope readers check out your program's website at yellandtell.com.

Denise Hughes—thank you for your valuable creative insight and helping me come up with a "Plan B" for the book title that ended up being better than "Plan A."

Kelly Mooney—I appreciate you making time during the holidays to do such a great photo shoot.

I would especially like to thank my supporters who have visited my website at kathleenterner.com, cheered me on via Facebook, or contacted me through my webpage. A huge thank you in advance to any readers who feel inspired to write a positive review about my book. It is my deep and sincere hope that my words might be an encouragement to others, and I can think of no greater compliment than to read your wonderful feedback.

APPENDIX I

DAY BY DAY ITINERARY

Date   **Destination**

July 1   Highlight—Country Mercantile
         Stayed—Pasco, Washington

July 2   Highlight—Bonner's Ferry
         Stayed—Bonner's Ferry, Idaho

July 3   Highlight—Glacier National Park
         Stayed—Kalispel, Montana

July 4   Highlight—Philipsburg and Anaconda Backroads
         Stayed— Butte, Montana

July 5   Highlight—Yellowstone National Park
         Stayed—Pray, Montana

July 6   Highlight—Yellowstone National Park
         Stayed—Pray, Montana

July 7   Highlight—Beartooth Pass
          Stayed—Red Lodge, Montana

July 8   Highlight—Rocket Motel
          Stayed—Custer, South Dakota

July 9   Highlight—Needles Highway, Wildlife Loop
          Stayed—Custer, South Dakota

July 10   Highlight—Iron Mountain Road
          Stayed—Custer, South Dakota

July 11   Hihglight—Bridal Veil Falls
          Stayed—Custer, South Dakota

July 12   Highlight—IBA Saddle Sore
          Stayed—St. Joseph, Michigan

July 13   Highlight—IBA Bun Burner
          Stayed—Niagara Falls, New York

July 14   Highlight—Niagara Falls, New York
          Stayed—Niagara Falls, New York

July 15   Highlight—Amish Country
          Stayed—Lancaster, Pennsylvania

July 16   Highlight—Time with Ethan
          Stayed—Washington, DC

July 17   Highlight— Time with Ethan
          Stayed—Washington, DC

July 18   Highlight—Time with Ethan
          Stayed—Washington, DC

July 19   Highlight—Time with Ethan
          Stayed— Washington, DC

July 20   Highlight—Blue Ridge Parkway
          Stayed—Fancy Gap, Virginia

July 21 Highlight—Tail of the Dragon

Stayed—Robbinsville, North Carolina

July 22 Highlight—Cherahola Parkway

Stayed—Monterey, Tennessee

July 23 Highlight—IBA Saddlesore

Stayed—Amarillo, Texas

July 24 Highlight—IBA Bun Burner

Stayed—Silverton, Colorado

July 25 Highlight—Million Dollar Highway

Stayed—Silverton, Colorado

July 26 Highlight—Telluride Loop

Stayed—Silverton, Colorado

July 27 Highlight—Black Canyon of the Gunnison
National Park

Stayed—Silverton, Colorado

July 28 Highlight—High Mountain Pies

Stayed—Leadville, Colorado

July 29 Highlight—Rocky Mountain National Park

Stayed—Estes Park, Colorado

July 30 Highlight—Rocky Mountain National Park

Stayed—Grand Lake, Colorado

July 31 Highlight—Red Stone Inn

Stayed—Redstone, Colorado

Aug 1   Highlight—Arches National Park

Stayed—Moab, Utah

Aug 2   Highlight—Canyonlands National Park

Stayed—Moab, Utah

Aug 3 Highlight—Mesa Verde National Park
       Stayed—Cortez, Colorado
Aug 4 Highlight—Capitol Reef National Park
       Stayed—Torrey, Utah
Aug 5 Highlight—Bryce Canyon National Park, Zion
       National Park
       Stayed—Springdale, Utah
Aug 6 Highlight—Zion National Park
       Stayed—Kanab, Utah
Aug 7 Highlight—Grand Canyon
       Stayed—Kanab, Utah
Aug 8 Highlight—Vegas Heat
       Stayed—Tonopah, Nevada
Aug 9 Highlight—Highway 120, Tioga Pass
       Stayed—Lee Vining, California
Aug 10 Highlight—Yosemite National Park
       Stayed—Curry Villiage, California
Aug 11 Highlight—Glacier Point
       Stayed—Tulare, California
Aug 12 Highlight—Sequoia National Park
       Stayed—Tulare, California
Aug 13 Highlight—Conzumel Road, Marin Headlands
       Stayed—Mill Valley, California
Aug 14 Highlight—California Coast
       Stayed—Gualala, California
Aug 15 Highlight—California Coast
       Stayed—Garberville, California

Aug 16 Highlight—Honeydew
        Stayed—Eureka, California
Aug 17 Highlight—Oregon Coast
        Stayed—Brookings, Oregon
Aug 18 Highlight—Klammath Lake
        Stayed—Lakeview, Oregon
Aug 19 Highlight—Bend, Oregon
        Stayed—Bend, Oregon
Aug 20 Highlight—Rafting the Deschutes
        Stayed—Bend, Oregon
Aug 21 Highlight—Painted Hills National Monument
        Stayed—Baker City, Oregon
Aug 22 Highlight—Hells Canyon
        Stayed—Salt Lake City, Utah
Aug 23 Highlight—Nevada Desert
        Stayed—Susanville, Califonia
Aug 24 Highlight—Escaping the Flames
        Stayed—Creswell, Oregon
Aug 25 Highlight—Otter Crest Loop
        Stayed—West Linn, Oregon

APPENDIX II

Washington, Idaho, Montana, Wyoming, South Dakota, Minnesota, Wisconsin, Illinois, Indiana, Michigan, Ohio, Pennsylvania, New York, Maryland, West Virginia, Virginia, North Carolina, Tennessee, Arkansas, Oklahoma, Texas, New Mexico, Colorado, Utah, Arizona, Nevada, California, Oregon

Appendix III

California

Hume Lake Christian Conference Center Grill, Sequoia National Park

In-N-Out Burger, Gilroy

Parkside Café, Stinson Beach

Roadhouse 99, Kingsburg

Colorado

Back Country Café, Gunnison

Backdoor Grill, Steamboat Springs

Colordao Boy Southwest, Ourey

Eureka Station, Silverton

Freddy's Burgers, Grand Junction

High Mountain Pies, Leadville

Moose's Chocolates, Ourey

Penelope's Old Time Burgers, Estes Park

Montana

Chico Hot Springs Dining Room, Pray

Piccola Cucina, Red Lodge

North Carolina

Tapoco Lodge, Robbinsville

Oregon

Creswell Bakery, Creswell

In-N-Out Burger, Grants Pass

Jackson's Corner, Bend

Mattie's Pancake House, Brookings

Pig 'N' Pancake, Newport

Pennsylvania

Callaloo, Lancaster

Tennessee

Tellico Grains Bakery, Tellico Plains

Utah

Blu Pig, Moab

Capitol Reef Inn and Café, Torrey

Patio Diner, Blanding

Virginia

Spelunkers, Front Royal

Washington

St. John's Bakery, Goldendale

Country Mercantile, Pasco

Appendix IV

Map of Route

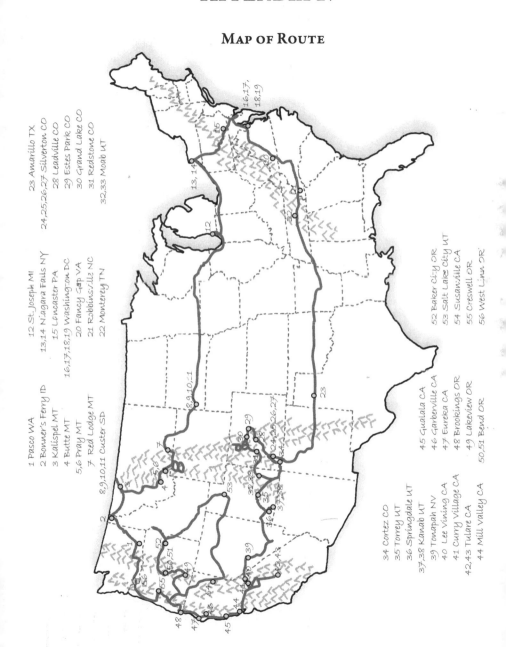

1 Pasco WA
2 Bonner's Ferry ID
3 Kalispel MT
4 Butte MT
5,6 Pray MT
7 Red Lodge MT
8,9,10,11 Custer SD

12 St. Joseph MI
13,14 Niagara Falls NY
15 Lancaster PA
16,17,18,19 Washington DC
20 Fancy Gap VA
21 Robbinsville NC
22 Monterey TN

23 Amarillo TX
24,25,26,27 Silverton CO
28 Leadville CO
29 Estes Park CO
30 Grand Lake CO
31 Redstone CO
32,33 Moab UT

34 Cortez CO
35 Torrey UT
36 Springdale UT
37,38 Kanab UT
39 Tonopah NV
40 Lee Vining CA
41 Curry Village CA
42,43 Tulare CA
44 Mill Valley CA

45 Gualala CA
46 Garberville CA
47 Eureka CA
48 Brookings OR
49 Lakeview OR
50,51 Bend OR

52 Baker City OR
53 Salt Lake City UT
54 Susanville CA
55 Creswell OR
56 West Linn OR

Also from Road Dog Publications

Those Two Idiots![12] *by A. P. Atkinson*
Mayhem, mirth, and adventure follow two riders across two continents. Setting off for Thailand thinking they were prepared, this story if full of mishaps and triumphs. An honest journey with all the highs and lows, wins and losses, wonderful people and low-lifes, and charms and pitfalls of the countries traveled through.

Motorcycles, Life, and . . .[12] *by Brent Allen*
Sit down at a table and talk motorcycles, life and . . . (fill in the blank) with award winning riding instructor and creator of the popular "Howzit Done?" video series, Brent "Capt. Crash" Allen. Here are his thoughts about riding and life and how they combine told in a lighthearted tone.

The Elemental Motorcyclist[12] *by Brent Allen*
Brent's second book offers more insights into life and riding and how they go together. This volume, while still told in the author's typical easy-going tone, gets down to more specifics about being a better rider.

A Short Ride in the Jungle[12] *by Antonia Bolingbroke-Kent*
A young woman tackles the famed Ho Chi Minh Trail alone on a diminutive pink Honda Cub armed only with her love of Southeast Asia, its people, and her wits.

Mini Escapades around the British Isles[12] *by Zoë Cano*
As a wonderful compilation of original short stories closer to home, Zoë Cano captures the very essence of Britain's natural beauty with eclectic travels she's taken over the years exploring England, Ireland, Scotland, and Wales.

Bonneville Go or Bust [1][2] by Zoë Cano
A true story with a difference. Zoë had no experience for such a mammoth adventure of a lifetime but goes all out to make her dream come true to travel solo across the lesser known roads of the American continent on a classic motorcycle.

I loved reading this book. She has a way of putting you right into the scene. It was like riding on the back seat and experiencing this adventure along with Zoë.—★★★★ Amazon Review

Southern Escapades [1][2] by Zoë Cano
As an encore to her cross country trip, Zoë rides along the tropical Gulf of Mexico and Atlantic Coast in Florida, through the forgotten backroads of Alabama and Georgia. This adventure uncovers the many hidden gems of lesser known places in these beautiful Southern states.

. . . Zoë has once again interested and entertained me with her American adventures. Her insightful prose is a delight to read and makes me want to visit the same places.—★★★★★ Amazon Review

Chilli, Skulls & Tequila [1][2] by Zoë Cano
Zoe captures the spirit of beautiful Baja California, Mexico, with a solo 3 000 mile adventure encountering a myriad of surprises along the way and unique, out-of-the-way places tucked into Baja's forgotten corners.

Zoe adds hot chilli and spices to her stories, creating a truly mouth-watering reader's feast!—★★★★ Amazon Review

Hellbent for Paradise [1][2] by Zoë Cano
The inspiring—and often nail-biting—tale of Zoë's exploits roaming the jaw-dropping natural wonders of New Zealand on a mission to find her own paradise.

Shiny Side Up [1][2] by Ron Davis
A delightful collection of essays and articles from Ron Davis, Associate Editor and columnist for *BMW Owners News*. This book is filled with tales of the road and recounts the joys and foibles of motorcycle ownership and maintenance. Read it and find out why Ron is a favorite of readers of the *Owners News*!

Beads in the Headlight [1] by Isabel Dyson
A British couple tackle riding from Alaska to Tierra del Fuego two-up on a 31 year-old BMW "airhead." Join them on this epic journey across two continents.

A great blend of travel, motorcycling, determination, and humor. —★★★★★
Amazon Review

Morocco Road [1][2] by Ragnar Hojland Espinosa
The author has big dreams of a round-the-world ride, but reality makes him rethink the huge scope of that endeavor, and he truncates his dream for the time being, but instead "gets his feet wet" on the dusty roads of Morocco trying this thing they call "adventure travel."

Chasing America [1][2] by Tracy Farr
Tracy Farr sets off on multiple legs of a motorcycle ride to the four corners of America in search of the essence of the land and its people.

In Search of Greener Grass [1] by Graham Field
With game show winnings and his KLR 650, Graham sets out solo for Mongolia & beyond. Foreword by Ted Simon

Eureka [1] by Graham Field
Graham sets out on a journey to Kazahkstan only to realize his contrived goal is not making him happy. He has a "Eureka!" moment, turns around, and begins to enjoy the ride as the ride itself becomes the destination.

Different Natures [1] by Graham Field
The story of two early journeys Graham made while living in the US, one north to Alaska and the other south through Mexico. Follow along as Graham tells the stories in his own unique way.

Thoughts on the Road [1][2] by Michael Fitterling
The Editor of *Vintage Japanese Motorcycle Magazine* ponders his experiences with motorcycles and riding and how they've intersected and influenced his life.

Northeast by Northwest[1][2] by Michael Fitterling
The author finds two motorcycle journeys of immense help staving off depression and the other effects of stress. Along the way, he discovers the beauty of North America and the kindness of its people.

. . . one of the most captivating stories I have read in a long time. Truly a MUST read!!—★★★★★ Amazon Review

Hit the Road, Jac![1][2] by Jacqui Furneaux
At 50, Jacqui leaves her home and family, buys a motorcycle in India, and begins a seven-year world-wide journey with no particular plan. Along the way she comes to terms with herself and her family.

Asphalt & Dirt[1][2] by Aaron Heinrich
A compilation of profiles of both famous figures in the motorcycle industry and relatively unknown people who ride, dispelling the myth of the stereotypical "biker" image.

A Tale of Two Dusters & Other Stories[1][2] by Kirk Swanick
In this collection of tales, Kirk Swanick tells of growing up a gearhead behind both the wheels of muscle cars and the handlebars of motorcycles and describes the joys and trials of riding

Man in the Saddle[1][2] by Paul van Hoof
Aboard a 1975 Moto Guzzi V7, Paul starts out from Alaska for Ushuaia. Along the way there are many twists and turns, some which change his life forever. English translation from the original Dutch.